STONE HEART
LIGHT HEART

THE INTELLIGENCE OF SELF MASTERY

Stella Petrou Concha

Copyright © 2021 Stella Petrou Concha

All rights reserved, except as permitted under the *Australian Copyright Act 1968*. No part of this publication may be reproduced, distributed, or transmitted in any form or by any means, including photocopying, recording, or other electronic or mechanical methods, without the prior written permission of the publisher, except in the case of brief quotations embodied in critical reviews and certain other noncommercial uses permitted by copyright law.

Every effort has been made to trace and seek permission for the use of the original source material used within this book. Where the attempt has been unsuccessful, the publisher would be pleased to hear from the author/publisher to rectify any omission.

First published in 2021 by Hambone Publishing
Melbourne, Australia

Editing by Mish Phillips, Stephanie Ayres and Emily Stephenson
Internal design by Jenelyn Leonor

For information about this title, contact:
Stella Petrou Concha
www.stellapetrouconcha.com.au

ISBN 978-1-922357-18-2 (paperback)
ISBN 978-1-922357-19-9 (ebook)

For Sofia and Alegra
Love Mum

The journey of self mastery is taking information and turning it into knowledge, taking knowledge and turning it into wisdom, and taking wisdom and turning it into intelligence.

- **Stella**

Contents

Introduction		xi
Your Book Map		xiii
One:	**The Canvas of Your Mind**	1
	Your Values Tree	6
	The Anatomy of the Brain	10
	Who's in Charge – You or the Zoo?	12
	Massey's Stages of Development	15
SECTION ONE: STONE HEART		**25**
Two:	**Awakening Stone Heart**	27
	Awareness Rising	28
	How the Canvas of Your Mind Dictates Your Behaviours	32
	The Power Of Detachment	36
	The Curse of People-Pleasing	42
	Taking Feedback Without Accepting Judgment	45
Three:	**Strengthening Stone Heart**	53
	What Is Strengthening Stone Heart?	54
	Strengthen Stone Heart by Embracing the Law of Failure	56
	Bounce	63

	Forgiveness	66
	When Life Keeps Repeating the Same Challenge	70
	How to Use Your Courage	71
Four:	**Accelerating Stone Heart**	**77**
	What Is Accelerating Stone Heart	78
	Accelerate Stone Heart by Creating Your Own Reality	79
	Your Word is Your Wand	81
	Mantras	85
	Habits = Discipline + Hard Work	87
Five:	**Leading with Stone Heart**	**95**
	What Is Leading with Stone Heart?	96
	Lead with Stone Heart by Energising from Within	98
	Taming the Animals in the Office	100
	The Power of Perspective	103
SECTION TWO: LIGHT HEART		**113**
Six:	**Awakening Light Heart**	**115**
	What Is Light Heart?	116
	Awaken Light Heart by Embracing the Present Moment	118
	Know Thyself	119
	Accept the Present	127

	Escape the Trap of Happiness	129
	Breathe In	131
	Awaken the Inner Wisdom	134
Seven:	**Strengthening Light Heart**	**139**
	What Is Strengthening Light Heart	140
	Beingness	143
	Embrace Life and Find Joy	147
	Passion and Empowered Action	149
Eight:	**Accelerating Light Heart**	**153**
	What Is Accelerating Light Heart?	154
	Living by the Laws of the Universe	155
	Manifesting Your Own Future	163
Nine:	**Leading with Light Heart**	**169**
	What Is Leading with Light Heart?	170
	Find the Inner Space	172
	The Frequency of Leadership	173
	Be the Chosen Chief	176
SECTION THREE: POWER		**183**
Ten:	**Power**	**185**
	Finding Power Through Purpose	187
	What if You Could?	192

Introduction

My father fought in the war against the Turkish invasion of Cyprus in 1974. During his four years of service, the country and its economy were annihilated. As his village was taken over by the hostile Turkish army, he, along with his five siblings, became a refugee. He was forced to work in Syria, sending money back to his war-torn family to support their recovery. By the age of 25, he'd given Cyprus the best part of his years, and he hated all that it stood for. When, in 1978, he met my mother, an Aussie-born Cypriot holidaying in Cyprus, he saw hope in a new challenge: migration.

Fast-forward fourteen years, and my father was bored. He spoke broken English and couldn't read or write. One Sunday, he had a fight with Mum, and she said, "Go to the library and learn how to read; go do something with yourself!". He went to Wallsend Library in Newcastle and came home that afternoon with a book, which we read together: *Bring Out the Magic in Your Mind*, by Al Koran. That day marked the beginning of my journey into learning about the *I* in me. That day changed my life.

I read that book as a child, and I still consider it my greatest gift. Everything I read, I applied. Everything I read, I practised. Everything I read, I believed.

The book taught me to write affirmations and say them over and over. It taught me that whatever I affirm becomes my reality. It taught me that my imagination has the power to conceive just about anything – and so long as it's possible in my thoughts, it can be possible in reality.

Pretty out-there stuff for a 12-year-old, hey? I dedicated my teenage years to learning about the mind, with a burning desire to master the *I* in me. By the age of 20, I'd read piles of mind-power books by many of the legends we laud today, and I had completed the Bob Proctor series *You Are Born Rich*. By 21, I was a master practitioner and trainer of neuro-linguistic programming (NLP).

This book is the culmination of 25 years of research and practice.

Learning about *I* and mastering Stone Heart, Light Heart must begin with understanding the canvas you call your mind.

Your Book Map

Stone Heart, Light Heart is written in three sections. Each section will take you on a journey through layers of learning. It is intended to be read first in a linear fashion; the concepts in Chapter One lay the foundation for the concepts in Chapter Two, and so on. Once you have read the book from cover to cover, you can then flick back to any particular point of interest and understand it deeply without needing to go back to the beginning.

Section One, *Stone Heart*, is all about mastering your mind. It's easy for your ego to cloud your presence with stories and judgments, making it near impossible to connect with your inner *I*. Stone Heart teaches you to master the greatest challenge of the mind by identifying and controlling the ego.

Section Two, *Light Heart*, is about turning in, finding *I*, and mastering your connection to your higher conscious mind. Finding *I* is not easy. Most of us will battle with the ego as we move closer to being present. Most people can't hold their presence without a thought of the past or a fantasy of the future. But the *I* within you cannot be found in thought! Let's go on a step-by-step journey to finding *I*. You might be surprised by what's in store!

Sections One and Two both follow a similar structure. They can each be broken up into four stages of learning: *awakening, strengthening, accelerating,* and *leading*.

The *awakening* stage brings your awareness to the mind and self, and encourages understanding based on knowledge and evidence.

The *strengthening* stage is about building the Stone Heart, Light Heart muscle. It involves growth, leaning into the hard stuff and facing the truth in the mirror.

The *accelerating* stage teaches you to amplify Stone Heart, Light Heart in your daily practice.

The *leading* stage addresses the application of Stone Heart, Light Heart in leadership, both generally and for you personally.

At the end of each chapter, you will have the opportunity to complete an exercise designed to help you integrate your learnings.

Section Three, *Power*, is short and sharp. It combines the learnings from the previous two sections. As you master Stone Heart, Light Heart, you awaken your power.

Let's take a walk through each chapter in preparation for the journey ahead.

In Chapters One and Two, we will uncover the science behind the canvas of your mind. You must understand the foundation of your mind before you can learn to govern as its ruling authority. Most people let their mind be run by others – family, institutions, social media – and I believe this is the primary reason why poor mental health is as prolific as it is. Here I will introduce you to the boundaries of your ego and teach you how to detach from the ego's core behaviours – behaviours such as judgment of self, judgment of others, and people pleasing.

Chapter Three will teach you how to strengthen your detachment from ego. It starts with embracing the law of failure to recover from life's great mishaps. Many people struggle to bounce back from big challenges, never building their internal emotional muscle of resilience. This chapter will awaken you to the joy of failure and reframe your mind towards embracing life's great learnings.

Once you have built the courage to fail and the resilience to bounce back from failure, Chapter Four will ask you to accelerate this learning by facing the truth in the mirror and recognising the aspects of you that need to be fine-tuned. You will be asked to take some serious responsibility for your thoughts, as your thoughts govern your inner world, and your inner world manifests in your outer world. At this point, it's all in your hands.

In Chapter Five, I will share how enlightened leaders create and govern the energy of their team. They need no one to derive their energy from; they energise themselves from within. Leaders who practise Stone Heart understand that their own inner worlds (thoughts and emotions) determine their impact as leaders.

Chapter Six marks the beginning of Section Two; you'll notice the change of pace. Here we will begin our journey to awaken Light Heart. The concepts will become undeniably deep-thinking as we begin to explore elements of the soul and consciousness.

Chapter Seven is about bringing acceptance into the present moment. This chapter will teach you how to build a relationship with the present by mastering happiness and sadness and finding joy in both.

Chapter Eight will bring forward the laws that govern our spirit and energetic world – the world in which the *I* resides. We will delve into the mysteries of life and uncover some of the overarching laws of the universe.

In Chapter Nine we will explore how Light Heart will empower you as a leader as you learn that your leadership is experienced through your frequency. You will discover how to create space mentally and energetically, and achieve complete mastery over your energy centres.

Chapter Ten comprises Section Three, *Power*. It rounds out the learnings of *Stone Heart* and *Light Heart* in one place. Here you will bring together everything you have learned to master your time and find your purpose.

Stone Heart, Light Heart is not just the title of this book, it's a way of being. Before you continue reading, I have three questions for you:

Do you know who you are?

Do you like who you are?

Are you the master of your life?

Chances are, your answers contained at least one 'No'. Don't worry, that will change. This book is your step-by-step guide towards three enthusiastic yeses!

By applying yourself to learning and understanding the concepts contained within this book, you will find your personal sense of self and finally answer the question, "Who am I?".

Your inner world is reflected in your outer world. If you want to make a change in your outer world, change your inner world.

Chapter 1

The Canvas of Your Mind

"Progress is impossible without change; and those who cannot change their minds cannot change anything."

George Bernard Shaw

The day my father came home with *Bring Out the Magic in Your Mind* was pivotal; it began my lifelong love affair with finding *I*. My age was significant: 12-year-olds don't question authors like an adult might. As a child you take anything published as gospel. I lacked the scepticism that might have hijacked my experience had it taken place a few years later. My mind was open to new concepts, so I was able to apply them without complication. My formative years were my training years, in which I tested different ideas like affirmations, mantras, meditations with crystals, and oracle cards. I made up my own mind about these various modalities through curiosity and experience.

For you, it will likely be more difficult (assuming you aren't a lucky 12-year-old who stumbled accidentally upon this book!). You will have to work hard to let go of your existing beliefs and assumptions and open your mind to absorb these new concepts.

Before we can explore this further, I need to take you through the basics of neuroscience. I need you to get to know your three minds (yes, three!) from a scientific perspective. Reflecting on your biological self is the first step towards mastering the vehicle of your mind.

The canvas of your mind is made up of three components:

- ❖ Your unconscious mind
- ❖ Your conscious mind
- ❖ Your higher conscious mind.

THE CANVAS OF YOUR MIND

Figure 1. The NLP perspective of your mind

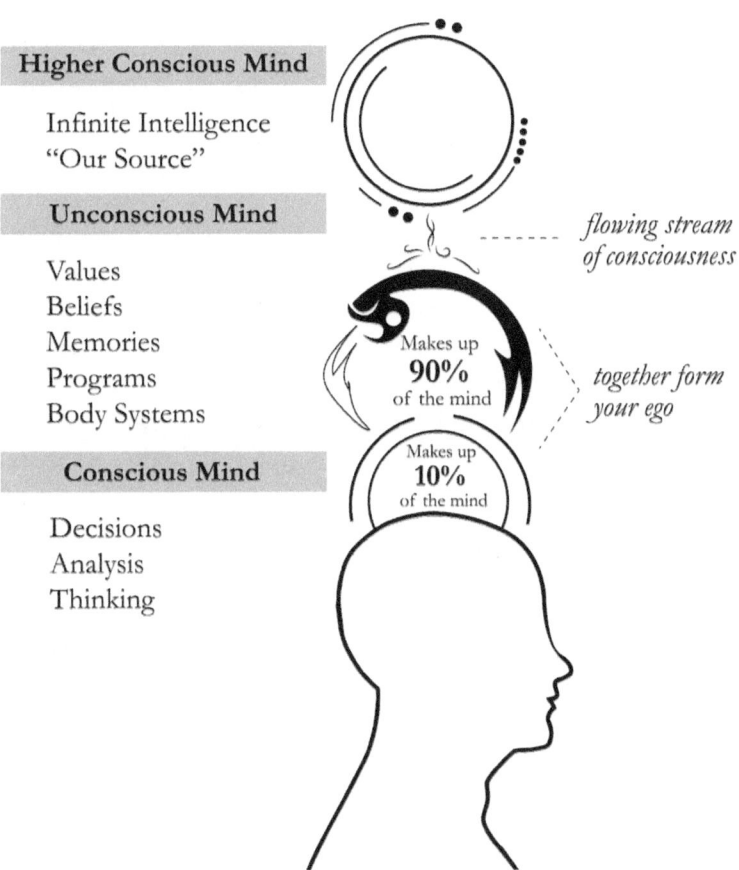

Your unconscious mind

You are born with a fully functioning unconscious mind. And it accounts for around 90% of your brain activity. Your unconscious mind is the part that runs your body without you having to think about it. It's the part that regulates your body's physiological systems, keeping them in perfect harmony. It keeps your heart beating, cleanses your blood, tells you when you're hungry, and fights off disease. Your unconscious mind is the computer system in charge of the most magnificent machine known to man – the human body.

Your unconscious mind stores all your memories – every single one. Even if your conscious mind doesn't remember, your unconscious mind does. It's also where all your values and beliefs live. Your unconscious value systems are built upon the values of your parents. If you were born into a religious family, for example, the values and beliefs of that religion are impressed upon your unconscious mind early in life. And if you're like most people, you'll follow those values for the rest of your life.

Unless, of course, you have an enquiring mind and realise as you become an adult that you have *choices* as to what you value and believe. You can *change* your values and beliefs. But how? That's where the challenge comes in. If your values and beliefs are unconscious, how on earth do you begin to change them? Don't worry, we'll get to that!

Your conscious mind

Your conscious mind is the part that thinks, uses critical judgment, and makes rational decisions. It's the analytical side of you, the side that knows wrong from right. It's the critic and the judge. It's the part that keeps you safe and out of harm's way (well, for the most part!).

THE CANVAS OF YOUR MIND

It takes around 21 years for the conscious mind to be developed. That's why the legal drinking age in America is 21. It's also why active parenting is so important. As children we struggle to make competent decisions because we're not yet capable of exercising full conscious awareness. That's why a two-year-old can easily become Superman and jump off a veranda without fear.

The conscious mind accounts for only 10% of your mind. It is, however, the 'big brother' to the unconscious mind, in that the unconscious mind is an obedient listener to the conscious mind. If the conscious mind sees a bear, for example, it communicates "Danger!" to your unconscious, and in turn your unconscious floods your body with adrenaline via the fight/flight/freeze response. Your unconscious mind is the computer system running the body, but your conscious mind is the person pushing all the buttons, see figure 2.

Figure 2.

Your Higher Conscious Mind

Your higher conscious mind is the wisdom inside you that is connected to all that is. It's where faith lives. It's where spirit lives. It's where God lives, or the divine presence inside you. It's your true north, and it's connected to everyone else's true north. Your higher conscious mind is an all-encompassing canopy that sits above all consciousness, the aspect of ourselves that we connect to when we meditate.

In order to know our purpose in life and our reason for being, we must connect with and bring forth the contents of the higher conscious mind. As we move through this book, you will see that by building your Stone Heart (mastering your unconscious and conscious minds) and then Light Heart (awakening your connection to your higher consciousness mind), you will become extremely powerful.

Power is not force. Power is effortless flow. Power is the ability to love in the face of great suffering. Power is fully accepting and embracing the present moment as if it were the moment you had chosen. And the way to awaken that power is through Stone Heart, Light Heart. Without Stone Heart, Light Heart, your power will be driven more from ego than from spirit, and it will inevitably waver.

Your Values Tree

According to neuro-linguistic programming (NLP), values are important to us, and they determine how we spend our time.

In the context of this book, a value is not a cultural standard or a moral compass for what's good and just in society (after all, that is a judgment that depends on the society you live in).

Values are simply the things that motivate you – things like family, love, or money. They're the reason you get out of bed and do what you do.

Beliefs are the rules you have set up to fulfil your values. You'll likely have a set of beliefs that cluster around each value. So, for example, take the value of money. Beliefs around money might include "money is hard to earn and easy to spend" or "you can't do what you love *and* make money". Your values are largely given to you before the age of seven. Your belief systems are also well established at a young age, but continue to layer and grow as time goes on.

When I think about values and beliefs, I imagine values as the large branches of a tree and beliefs as the many smaller branches and foliage extending from them, see figure 3. When you put all your values and beliefs together, you have your very own 'values tree' – a system of neural networks that drives your behaviours and decisions.

You can see that if you change a few of your beliefs, you won't have any impact on the values they connect to. A large branch can easily survive snapping off a few smaller branches. If you want to shift a value, you need to cut off the entire limb – which means letting go of the whole cluster of beliefs that hang off that value.

So why would you *want* to change your values and beliefs?

Figure 3. The values tree

WHEN THE CANVAS OF OUR MIND DOESN'T SERVE US

Given that our values and beliefs are encoded at such a young age, it's hardly surprising that sometimes we can end up with values and beliefs that don't serve us.

Let me give you an example of how our unconscious mind and conscious mind play out in our behaviours. I grew up attending a gorgeous Christian school in Newcastle, where I learned some incredible values around discipline, respect, and kindness that I still hold dear. It was a typical private school: skirt below the knee, wide-brimmed hat, respect and no back chat, etc. This raft of behavioural rituals all funnelled into the values of discipline and respect. But I got one value from that school that really didn't serve me.

You see, my school was a strict Christian school, so we learned that if we had sex before marriage, we would go to Hell. We learned that sex before marriage was a sin (and a bad one, at that). I was very scared of sex, because I was very scared of Hell, and in my mind the two were inextricably linked. This fear was so damaging to my psyche and emotions that it took me the best part of my early twenties to unpick it and restack it with new beliefs that served me. Because it wasn't just the value itself that had ingrained itself in my unconscious mind, but the whole belief tree that stacked around it – the foliage of belief systems growing from that value stem.

My unconscious mind didn't just learn that sex was bad. It learned that if I had sex before I was married, I was going to Hell. It learned that sex is a sin. Can you imagine how damaging these beliefs were to my emotions and psyche? More serving beliefs might have been "Sex is wonderful with a person you love" or "Sex can be hurtful when it's with someone you don't love".

Whenever my brain considered sex and where I stood on the topic, the fear of Hell would surface. I had the most vicious nightmares about the devil. The more I thought about sex, the more nightmares I had. I still had not had sex, and I was certain that if I did open my legs, I would erupt in flames and grow horns.

My curiosity about how I was feeling, along with my training in values and beliefs, gave me the opportunity to understand where these thoughts were coming from. I became my own psychologist. I had learned the tools to rewire my thinking and my beliefs. So rather than succumbing to the low-level beliefs residing in my unconscious, I worked to understand how they'd got there. And before long, I began to empower myself to form new beliefs which would serve me better. I did have sex before I got married. I did not go to Hell. And I am in a loving and successful marriage. I changed my belief tree.

We all have our own personal values and belief trees. We have values around everything from health to career, from family to finances. And attached to each value is a series of beliefs. These beliefs form the part of you that I call the ego. This is the part of you that you have learned over time, and it can change from moment to moment. Your system of values and beliefs is essential to who you are, but it is not the *I* within you.

THE ANATOMY OF THE BRAIN

To awaken Stone Heart, Light Heart, you need to understand the curse of the mind – the shortcomings of the tool you are playing with. And this starts with understanding the anatomy of the brain.

Your brain can be divided into three parts, as shown below: the reptile brain, the limbic brain, and the neocortex.

Figure 4. The anatomy of the brain

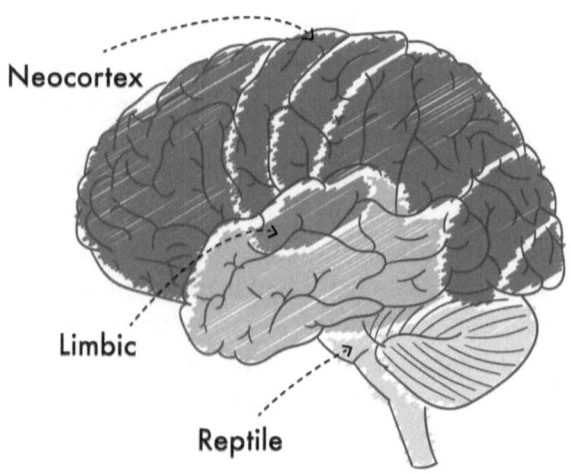

THE CANVAS OF YOUR MIND

YOUR REPTILE BRAIN (UNCONSCIOUS)

Your reptile brain, consisting of the cerebellum and the brainstem, is the oldest part of your brain, evolutionarily speaking. This is the most basic and essential part of the brain, the part that keeps you alive. Reptilian thinking is all about survival. I call it the zoo, because it controls the animal part of us.

The reptile brain:

- ❖ controls the body's vital organs — heart rate, breathing, body temperature, balance, etc.
- ❖ is all about survival.

YOUR LIMBIC BRAIN (UNCONSCIOUS)

Your limbic brain, consisting of the hippocampus, the amygdala, and the hypothalamus, is the source of your unconscious and bias judgments and has a strong influence on your behaviour.

Your limbic brain:

- ❖ controls emotions
- ❖ creates the fight/flight/freeze response
- ❖ stores all your memories
- ❖ generates arousal
- ❖ detects fear
- ❖ accepts limits
- ❖ determines your comfort zone.

YOUR NEOCORTEX (CONSCIOUS)

The neocortex, consisting of the two large cerebral hemispheres at the front of the brain, has grown over hundreds of thousands of years, gradually developing the capacity for language, abstract thinking, creative imagination, and higher consciousness – all the things that set us apart as humans. The highly developed neocortex is highly flexible and has an inexhaustible ability to learn.

Your neocortex:

- ❖ enables higher functions such as sensory perception
- ❖ generates motor command
- ❖ enables spatial reasoning
- ❖ is responsible for conscious thought
- ❖ is responsible for language
- ❖ is where intelligence lives.

Who's in Charge – You or the Zoo?

With multiple parts of the mind operating in different ways, the questions bear asking: what mind are you using to solve our more complex challenges? Who is really in charge? Is it you or the zoo?

When the zoo takes over

From a scientific standpoint, living with stress is living in survival mode – and as we just learned, that means the reptile and limbic brains are in control. When we perceive stressful circumstances that threaten us in some way, our primitive nervous system kicks into gear and our body mobilises enormous amounts of energy to kick us into a new gear: fight, flight, or freeze. We all know the feeling: racing heart, dilated pupils, a rush of glucose and hormones into the bloodstream. The body gets ready to move.

The challenge for the modern human is that our stressors are not the same as those of our ancestors. We don't have a lot of physical stressors; rather, our stressors are often related to relationships, money, career, kids. Aspects of life where fighting, fleeing, or freezing are really not likely to serve us well! Rather, many of today's stressors require emotional intelligence to solve. The limbic response that served our ancestors so well really doesn't cut it for the types of challenges we face today.

THE MONKEY MIND AND THE EGO

Throughout this book you'll hear me referencing the 'monkey mind'. The monkey mind is the combination of your reptilian brain and your limbic brain — the animal parts of you. When you're operating from your monkey mind, it's like being in the zoo!

Buddhists believe that the monkey mind is essentially the construct, or outcome, of your ego. So when you're not in control of your ego, when you're not aware of it, you're in monkey mind. This shows up as randomly applying feelings and thoughts to situations rather than applying logic and emotional intelligence to act thoughtfully.

But hold on a second — what exactly is the ego?

Ego is, simply put, your sense of self. It is the self-perception you have built over time and it carries with it all your values, beliefs, filters, and unconscious modi operandi. It's the framework through which you interpret the world. And it's governed by your monkey mind.

Most people have a negative perspective or understanding of ego. Phrases like "He has a big ego" or "I don't really have an ego" give a false impression of what ego really is. They indicate firstly that ego is something we may or may not have, and secondly that it is something we should avoid. Only arrogant, self-serving people have egos, right?

Wrong! Ego is so often used as a judgment, yet this is a complete misinterpretation of the word. Certainly, arrogance might be a behavioural outcome of your ego, but so might shame, sadness, or guilt. Yet you don't hear people using the word ego when they're talking about someone who is sad!

The truth is, we all have an ego. It's just a fact. Our job is to acknowledge it, realise we can change it, and master it. To shift from animal thinking to control thinking.

Understanding the construct of the ego and its relationship to the monkey mind is vital in order to begin to take control of your ego. You can't get rid of it, and nor should you want to – but you can prevent it from controlling you. And in Chapter Two, you'll learn how.

Figure 5. The monkey mind

THE CANVAS OF YOUR MIND

Massey's Stages of Development

In neuro-linguistic programming training, we learn about sociologist Morris Massey's four stages of development[1]. We are concerned with the first three, as shown here:

Figure 6.

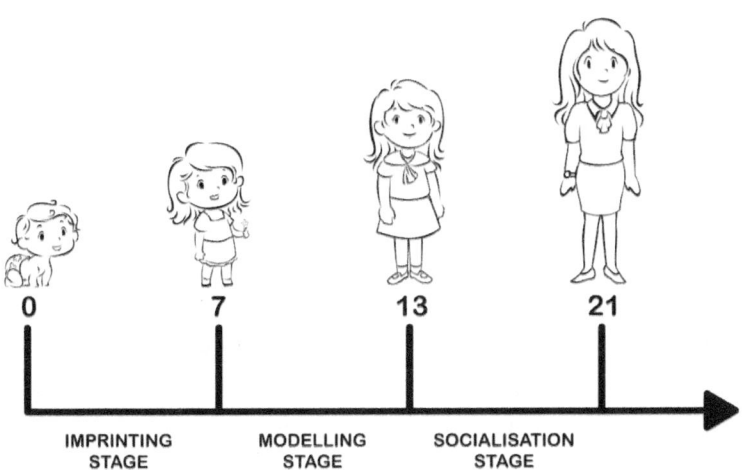

These stages reflect the stages of growth the conscious mind goes through before reaching full maturity at the age of roughly 21. Reflecting on how the significant events across your life relate to these stages can give you some insight into the canvas of your mind.

Imprinting stage (age 0–7)

All of your values and beliefs are imprinted on your unconscious mind by your seventh birthday. They come directly from the people who rear you and/or whom you trust. For most of us, that's our parents. They are also shaped by the events that happen to you. Consider your earliest years. Was there a divorce? A winning lottery ticket? The birth of a sibling? A car accident? A big move? Such events, and people's handling of them, are imprinted on your unconscious mind, shaping your values and beliefs. Sadly, some of those values and beliefs are bound to be problematic.

Imagine having a blank pizza base from which to build your ultimate pizza (for me, that's the diavola). Your mind is a blank pizza base when you are born. By the time you are seven, the majority of the toppings have been put on. Your pizza now has a flavour, a distinct character. We think that's it, that the pizza is finished! But it doesn't have to be. If you're not happy with your pizza, you can always go back and pick the toppings off. The same applies to your values tree. If you don't like the values tree that has grown in your unconscious mind, you'll need to go all the way back to your childhood and unpick the beliefs you acquired back then. When I coach and work with leaders, I pay a lot of attention to early childhood, because it forms the building blocks for all subsequent life decisions.

MODELLING STAGE (AGE 8–13)

Between the ages of eight and thirteen, you go through a modelling period, where you imitate behaviours of those around you. My best friend at that age was a disabled girl called Kelly. She was my best friend for 25 years before she died of a heart attack when I was 30. Kelly had spina bifida. She could barely walk, but she got along okay with assistance. When I was eight, I wanted to be like Kelly. I certainly didn't judge her for her disability; I just thought she was super cool. So I began to walk like her. With conscious intention, I started to walk with a significant limp and sway. This is typical behaviour from a child at this age. Monkey see, monkey do!

Why does this matter? Well, the impressions your brain receives during your modelling period don't only shape your behaviours at the time, they persist well into adulthood. If your parents are musical, music will have a place in your life, too. You might not be musical per se, but music will still be imprinted on your brain as something that you feel drawn to model in some way or form. On a more sinister level, if your parents are violent, domestic violence is more likely to occur in your home as an adult. It goes without saying that this kind of tendency is something we would do well to recognise.

Socialisation stage (age 14–21)

Between the ages of 14 and 21, you learn all you can about love and relationships. This is where we begin to test and learn about friendships, love, sex and everything else that simmers away in that hot pot of adolescence. When I work with adults who have challenges around relationships and love, I always track back to this period.

When I learned that sex before marriage was a sin, I didn't question that belief. I had no conscious awareness of the impact these lessons could have on our future relationships, and even if I had, I wasn't ready to challenge them. My conscious mind hadn't fully formed yet; I was still a teenager. So the experiences and beliefs that were bestowed on me during those years were hardwired into my adult operating system. As an adult, it became apparent that these beliefs about sex were ludicrous and unfair. But as a teenager, they had seemed entirely legitimate.

Why should this matter to you? Because relationships are the foundation for everything in life. Marriage, parenthood, social interaction, business management, career development... EVERYTHING!

Why is it important to understand the developmental stages?

Understanding Massey's developmental stages allows us to understand where our values have come from. In doing so, we give ourselves the perspective necessary to realise that *we are not our values*. Our values and beliefs can change. Having awareness and taking control of the canvas of your mind is stage one of self-mastery.

But how do you do this?

It takes humility and self-awareness to take control of the cockpit of your mind. And that's what we're going to develop in this book. Limbic and reptile brain dominance will prohibit you from enjoying the benefits of Stone Heart, Light Heart. The philosophy of Stone Heart, Light Heart comes from mastering all three of your minds. It is in awareness that you will find your immense power. It's important for you to continually look back on what you've learned about the canvas of your mind as you move through this journey of self-discovery. Is your canvas a mess of thorns and weeds, or a beautiful garden of thoughts?

Stone Heart, Light Heart in action

The first step to awakening Stone Heart is understanding the canvas of your mind and rewiring the unconscious beliefs that don't serve you. The following exercises will help you work towards that aim.

Reflect on the events that occurred in your life, and the people you spent most time with during each of your developmental stages. Consider the values and beliefs that formed as a result.

Under each of Massey's stages of development below, note the life events that may have contributed to your unconscious values and beliefs. Take some time to understand your canvas.

There really is no wrong or right here. There is only your truth.

Birth to 7 years old (imprinting stage – values and beliefs):

....

....

....

....

....

8 years old to 13 years old (modelling stage):

....
....
....
....
....

14 years old to 21 years old (socialisation stage):

....
....
....
....
....

Draw your values tree, with all the values you hold in life. Next, add in the beliefs that stem from those values. Think of as many beliefs as you can.

For example, for the value 'education', a belief might be 'I must go to university to be successful'.

Finally, take some time to reflect. Begin to explore the canvas of your mind more deeply. Which beliefs serve you, and which do not? Which beliefs need to change?

Remember, the beliefs you have are just the stories you tell yourself. They are not immutable truths.

Now redraw your values and beliefs tree with more resourceful values and beliefs. What beliefs do you wish you had instead? Would these new beliefs give you more desirable outcomes? A more desirable life?

SECTION ONE:
STONE HEART

I am not my thoughts

What I think I am, I am not

I once had a thought

Chapter 2

Awakening Stone Heart

"The greatest habit we must change is the habit of being ourselves."

Dr Joe Dispenza

Awareness Rising

When you read or talk to people around self-awareness, having an awakening, or becoming more conscious of who they are, many people talk about moments in their lives when they had a wake-up call. Often, moments like that are borne from trauma, disease, divorce – massive critical life events. But we don't have to have those massive critical life events to begin to understand who we are. Yes, those big critical life events are great opportunities for people to awaken. But you don't want to have to get cancer or go through a divorce to change your life!

This book is about taking the opportunity to learn about yourself, and allowing awareness of who you are to arise, bit by bit, layer by layer. (Self-)Awareness rising is about making a personal commitment. It means saying, "I'm committed to knowing who I am, where I've come from, and what I stand for. I will be the best I can be in the life I'm living now".

When you make that choice, you change your bearing in life. You take a different journey. It's a journey of getting to know yourself, of self-mastery. And the first step is simply to make the choice to allow awareness of who you are to begin to arise. The journey doesn't end, there's no destination. When you jump on this journey of self-mastery, what you're chasing is incremental awareness.

As you get to know yourself more, your power compounds. It's not a linear journey, and there's magic in that. Just when you feel like you're not making any progress, that may be the moment your growth accelerates exponentially. And when that happens, you'll see opportunities you'd only ever dreamt of.

What is Stone Heart?

Stone Heart is the awakening, strengthening, and accelerating of the mastery of your mind. Stone Heart is the behaviour or habit of awakening to the division between the ego and the *I*, understanding how to distinguish between them, and detaching from the ego.

Your values and beliefs form the lens through which you perceive the external world, but you were not born with these values and beliefs. So your perception isn't intrinsic to who you are; it's merely a framework you've developed over time based on extrinsic factors. And this framework can be changed. This fact is at the heart of the philosophy of Stone Heart.

Stone Heart is about recognising the malleability of your values and beliefs, and choosing to shape them for yourself. In this way, you can develop your own personal operating system. Your operating system will never be totally independent of your reptile and limbic brains, however. There will always be some degree of hormonal interference with the operating system you've built for yourself, contributing to your physical state and experience. And as you've learned, this interference can often be un-serving, producing unhelpful outcomes such as depression, anger, sadness, guilt or even disconnection from life. But by changing your operating system using the principles of Stone Heart, Light Heart, you can build your resilience to external factors and remain steadfast in the face of challenge.

The wisdom of Stone Heart, Light Heart paved my journey to mastering the mind, and it can do the same for you.

Why is stone heart so important?

What came first? The inner world or the outer world?

The answer is clear: your inner world drives your outer world. Your thoughts play out physiologically in your body. Your body then acts in certain ways, manifesting or creating different scenarios for you in your outer world.

If you want to understand a person's inner world, just watch their behaviours and you'll soon see what's happening on the inside.

> *My inner world is reflected in my outer world. If I want to make a change in my outer world, I must change my inner world.*

The quality of your inner thoughts is crucial. They are not invisible, and they are not meaningless. Your inner thoughts control your neurochemistry, your hormones, the entire network of chemicals that run your body. Your inner world is more impactful than your diet or your exercise habits.

You know, I actually used to get frustrated with the concept of manifestation. I would read old motivational books that told me that so long as I could conceive something in my mind, it must be possible, and I would bristle. I disliked these grandiose claims because it seemed to me that they weren't grounded in reality.

But in 2002, when I completed my studies in neuro-linguistic programming, I learned that, given that our basic physiological needs are met (which, considering among other things the education necessary for me to write this book and for you to read it, I feel I can assume to be the case here), we really are responsible for every piece of reality in our lives.

Since learning techniques to reprogram my mind and reorganise unconscious thought patterns, I have been able to transform my mind into my own beautiful masterpiece. A masterpiece that I have designed specifically for me, according to my true values and beliefs. My masterpiece might not resonate with your values and beliefs, and your masterpiece might not resonate with your friends' values and beliefs. We are all unique. I, for example, would never be a politician. Being in politics is not part of my dream, so I have not manifested it in my masterpiece. But if it's part of your dream, you can manifest it in yours. I have designed my life with conscious thought, and so can you.

Mastering Stone Heart will enable you to exist in your truest form. It will prevent unchecked impulses triggered by external factors – hormones, other people's opinions, beliefs you developed as a child – from controlling your reactions to life. Stone Heart provides the awareness necessary to distinguish your true self from everything else.

This distinction is the beginning of self-mastery. Why is self-mastery so important? Because the only thing you can control in life is yourself. We certainly can't control the environment. We can't control other people's choices, nor can we control their actions. We can, however, master the decisions that we ourselves make, the activities we participate in, and our responses to the external environment.

With the understanding that every member of the human race holds the capacity to master themselves, imagine the world we can create, the sustainability we can establish, the terror we can eradicate. In mastering ourselves, we foster harmony for all.

How the Canvas of Your Mind Dictates Your Behaviours

As we've already mentioned, to find *I*, you must start by understanding the canvas of your mind as it currently stands. Only then can you redesign your canvas, tailoring it to suit your true self. Your new canvas will then become the new basis for your unconscious thinking and therefore your day-to-day physiology and behaviour.

Of course, the question bears asking: How do we actually do this?

We do this by taking a look at the neuro-linguistic programming (NLP) model of communication[2]. In NLP we believe that when we know better, we do better. Here, we will unpack the science behind this think-and-create formula.

When you experience one of life's external events, that experience passes through a series of filters in your brain. These filters effectively reinterpret and judge the event according to your hierarchy of values and beliefs, your memories and past decisions, and what we call 'meta programs'. Meta programs are essentially internal sorting systems that help us decide what to pay attention to.

The filters shape our interpretation of an event in three main ways: they *distort* the event, *delete* some aspects of its context, and *generalise* it to broader contexts. The result is a highly personalised internal representation of that event. This internal image stimulates the limbic brain to give you an emotive response by pumping neuropeptides into your blood. That emotive response in turn causes a physical response, which plays out as your behaviour.

Figure 7. The NLP communication model

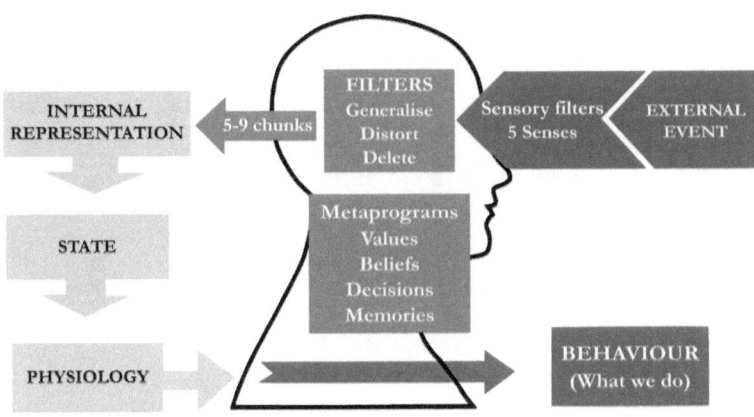

Let's unpack this simply. Say you have a phobia of spiders.

External event: Spider crawls over the outside of your windscreen as you get in the car.

Sensory perception: You see the spider.

Filters: Meta programs, values, beliefs, memories, and decisions.

Distort
- ❖ You feel a crawling sensation on your face.
- ❖ You think, "Spiders are scary and I am going to die if I don't kill it!"

Delete
- ❖ You forget the spider can't touch you, as it's outside the car.

❖ You disregard the fact that you've never actually been hurt by a spider.

Generalise
❖ You think there must be spiders hiding all over the car.
❖ You decide, "I'm catching a cab to work. I can never drive my car again!"

Internal representation: You think you have a spider crawling on your face, and that it is going to kill you.

State: You are terrified.

Emotive response: Your limbic brain stimulates release of adrenaline, activating your fight/flight/freeze response.

Physiology: Your body tenses up and you lose control of your limbs as they shake in response to the adrenaline.

Behaviour: At first you freeze up, then you force yourself to jump out of the car, still shaking with fear.

If this event happened to a seasoned gardener, it would pass through different filters, resulting in a different emotive response and therefore a different behaviour. Our behaviours vary based on the filters, programming, and architecture of our mind.

If you want to change your behaviours, you need to change the canvas of your mind. I'm thankful that I learned this very young, as it's given me the tools to be able to turn inward in order to create my outward reality. When I reflect back on my journey, I believe that these are critical concepts and tools that we should all be learning, whether it's in primary school, in high school, or as a mandatory subject in university degrees. All children and young adults should be taught how to master themselves before they get caught up in the whirlwind of adult life.

These concepts are fundamental to what it means to be human, and yet nobody teaches them. We learn how to perform complex algebra, how molecules interact with each other, how to critically analyse fiction… but we don't even learn the basics of how our own minds work. Learning these concepts should be considered a basic need, so that as we begin to navigate the real world, with all its difficulties and complexities, we have the tools to do it well – instead of ending up in our forties with a whole host of self-created challenges.

This is why it's so important to me to share Stone Heart, Light Heart with you. Fully embracing Stone Heart, Light Heart doesn't mean you won't have challenges – I still have a host of them! What it means is that you will have created a life based around your own choices, and you will take full responsibility and credit for those choices. You'll feel complete in the present moment, so that you experience enjoyment of life irrespective of the things that you have achieved or not achieved.

DEVELOP STONE HEART BY DETACHING FROM EGO

Every experience you go through changes your thinking a little, and along with it your beliefs and values. This change filters through to your ego, which in turn shapes your perceptions. As you experience life, your ego changes, and as your ego changes, your experience of life changes. But are you yourself changing? Or is it merely your perception of self – your ego?

When people go through divorce, disaster, or sickness, such a radical change to their external environment can change their perception. This in turn changes the construct of their ego, so that the way they experience life from then on changes, too. They often describe this as a wake-up call to the true meaning of life. Stone Heart allows us to experience the same awakening, but without the external pressure.

The first step in building Stone Heart is to become aware of your ego, and of when you're operating from your ego — which often means operating with no self-control at all. The two biggest behaviours that operate out of ego are attachment and judgment. Learning to perceive these behaviours in yourself, then, is the first step towards becoming aware of — and then detaching from — your ego.

THE POWER OF DETACHMENT

In order to understand the power of detachment, we must first come to grips with attachment. Your brain naturally attaches to ideas that support its belief system. It comes to see those ideas as fixed and unchangeable, and will often stubbornly argue the point even in the face of evidence to the contrary. When we're firmly attached to an idea, our brain's biased operating system obsessively supports and establishes that idea to the point that we can't see past it to even consider different ones.

Detachment, on the other hand, is the ability to hear and acknowledge other perspectives without considering them a threat to your own. Detachment allows you to hold your perspectives, but doesn't let them define who you are or how you respond. Detachment allows you, when appropriate, to change your perspectives to ones that are more accurate or serve you better.

In my twenties, I felt challenged by the dogma and judgments of religion. I was born into a Greek Orthodox family, which of course shaped my values and beliefs as a young adult. When Greek Orthodox Christians walk into church, they are asked to light a candle, make the sign of the cross in front of the icon of Mother Mary and Jesus, then kiss the icon. This is really a practice to stimulate one's mind to turn in, be present, and be ready to receive the word of God. One of the beliefs that the religion holds is that when a woman is menstruating, she cannot kiss the icons of Mother Mary and Jesus upon walking into the church because she is not clean.

As I got older, my inquisitive mind began to wonder on this. I was, and still am, pretty sure God isn't checking our pockets for tampons while we pray. So I decided to detach from the dogmas that had been controlling my mind and review the belief tree that I had created. I reflected carefully on the ideas I had become attached to, and I began to reshape my beliefs into a system that served me.

I love the traditions of my culture that encourage spiritual connection and oneness, but from time to time I see a furphy and it makes me smile. Maybe in the past, when women had poor sanitary systems, not walking into a public establishment while menstruating might have been considered a reasonable request. But 2000 years on, perhaps that rule no longer has the same relevance. Just because it's part of the belief system passed down by the church doesn't mean it has to be part of my own personal belief system. I can assess each idea on its own merits, because I am not blindly attached to any given idea.

Attachment to ideas is ludicrous, really. It is purely a constraint of one's ego. Holding onto ideas that reinforce our beliefs gives the illusion of control, but in reality it is quite the opposite. Attached, egoic thinking is linked to disempowerment. When you are attached to ideas and thoughts, you can't remain in control of your mind when those ideas come up. Rather than controlling your ideas, you allow your ideas to control you.

All fixed thinking is born from ego. When you cling blindly to your ideas and beliefs, it's as if you're letting a monkey do your thinking for you. Your ego has such a stronghold on your mind that it's become the president of your entire operating system. When a strong sense of ego commands your every action and decision, you are less likely to grow and find peace, because your decisions are not being made by your true, genuine self.

Detachment comes when you develop awareness of the ideas and thoughts you're connecting to as separate to yourself, which prevents you from forming un-serving emotional bonds to these ideas. Awareness of attachment is the beginning of detachment.

Detaching from Judgment

Being judged by others feels awful. In fact, even just listening to people gossiping and judging others feels awful. Imagine what you are doing to your body, mind, and soul when you perpetrate and maintain this cycle of judgment.

Detaching from the judgment of others is your first major accelerant in building your power. Judgments are essentially stories we tell ourselves to explain what we *think* has happened. These stories, no matter how invented they may be, become our truth as long as we remain controlled by our ego. Awakening Stone Heart involves detaching from these stories and making decisions from a deeper base within you.

Gossip is a telltale sign of attachment to judgment of others. In 2018, I was sitting by myself, having lunch at the MetCentre in Sydney, when I heard one of the women at the table next to me say about her work colleague, "What the hell is Sarah's problem today! Has she got attitude because her presentation was crap?" The judgment and attachment in her words opened up the floodgates for the most vile and worthless form of conversation: gossip. But I didn't feel sad for Sarah, I felt sad for the lady sitting beside me, because I could hear that she was entirely consumed by ego – dangerous territory for anyone seeking success. She was so attached to her own ego that she couldn't see Sarah for the human she was.

If the lady had cared at all about Sarah, she might have asked her privately, "Are you okay? You seem distracted today". As for the criticism of her "crap" presentation, comparative judgments are just further attachment to egoic thinking. She could have given Sarah direct, valuable feedback, perhaps explaining why the presentation hadn't connected with her, rather than making an empty judgment to someone who could do nothing about it. There is no power in that. When you behave in this way, you create a sense of dissonance. But you're creating dissonant energy not towards the person you're speaking ill of, but towards yourself. You're not sending your energy to the person you're judging. You're holding it. You're embodying it.

Awakening Stone Heart really starts with bringing awareness to your unconscious biases, especially towards others. Mastery of detachment from external judgment starts with catching yourself judging others, and stopping that judgment in its tracks. It will happen sometimes. It will happen all the time in the beginning! But as you build Stone Heart, you will master this detachment.

This does not mean you can't have an opinion! I have lots of opinions, but I am not attached to them and I am open to changing them. My opinions don't run my mind. And I don't have to judge those who see from a different viewpoint. We all have unique value trees and belief systems within our unconscious minds, built over time from our own unique upbringings. I may disagree with someone's behaviour, but I won't judge them for it.

Judging people locks you into your monkey mind, which causes you harm. Every time you pass a judgment on another human, it's like a boomerang that comes back and smacks you straight between the eyes. Your judgments consistently harm one person: you. In the absence of awareness, the judgment cycle deepens the divide between your ego and who you really are. It becomes harder and harder to find the *I* within as it becomes entangled in a matrix of thoughts and ideas. The true essence of who you are is smothered.

Imagine a political conversation happening between a left and a right-wing supporter, each with his own viewpoint. Conversations are opportunities for sharing such beliefs or viewpoints. An attached mind will argue a point and sometimes escalate it with judgment ("If you think that, you're an idiot!"). A difference in opinion quickly turns into a personal attack. This is the cycle of attachment and judgment in action. Each person's beliefs are so intertwined with their identity that they are unable to interact without judgment. A detached person, on the other hand, can have a viewpoint and converse without becoming emotional or judgmental. That viewpoint is not attached to who they are; it just happens to be their viewpoint today.

You are not your thoughts

So we begin to recognise the power in being detached from one's thoughts. We also see the power of not passing judgment (considering judgments are thoughts too).

> *I am not my thoughts.*
> *What I think I am, I am not.*
> *I once had a thought.*

As you read the above mantra, you may sense an apparent contradiction. Earlier we asserted that "Your inner thoughts control your neurochemistry, your hormones, the entire network of chemicals that run your body", yet here we have a mantra asserting, "I am not my thoughts". How can we hold both these concepts at the same time? Aren't they contradictory?

Actually, they're not. The two ideas may seem paradoxical, but when we look more closely, we can see that they operate in vastly different contexts. In the first, we are talking about deep, conscious, consistent decisions detached from ego. These are the 'thoughts' that dictate our physiology and give us the ability to create and manifest. In the second, we are referring merely to the flippant thoughts that pass through our minds without conscious intention. These 'thoughts' have no bearing on who we are.

These mantras are a tool for dealing with the flippant thoughts that we have moment to moment. One moment we're happy, the next moment we're sad. One moment it's all good, the next moment it's all bad. If you allow yourself to be dominated by these thoughts, you're operating out of the external rather than the internal. You're not in alignment with yourself.

Understand that your momentary thoughts or judgments are not who you are. The stories you run are not who you are. How can they be, when they are constantly changing?

My desire to awaken Stone Heart and bring my unconscious operating model into an empowered, aware state was the key driver that helped me to stop judging people. When I realised and accepted that judging people primarily hurts me, I stopped. It's very peaceful to practise non-judgment. And the peacefulness expands the less you judge. As your peace expands, so does your detachment. This gives you more space to enjoy and love life because you aren't so caught up in the monkey-mind cycle of judgment and attachment. This expansion of peace is Light Heart rising within you.

The Curse of People-Pleasing

If I had to pass judgment on myself, I'd say I have an unconscious people-pleasing habit. I've had to work extremely hard to rewire my unconscious habit of people pleasing. As a Greek-Cypriot woman, I've been taught almost from birth how to be a professional people-pleaser!

People pleasing involves continually trying to make others happy, even at your own expense. It stems from low self-worth and the need for approval. And it is centric to being a Greek-Cypriot woman!

On a hot day, you might crave a glass of cold water so badly that you guzzle it down, feeling the buzz of an endorphin boost that makes you say, "Aahhh! Nothing beats a glass of cold water!" ...but how long are you satisfied before you feel thirsty again? People pleasing is much the same. The desire for love and approval is the thirst, the pleasing is the glass of water. The thirst for approval can be temporarily satisfied by pleasing people, but it's just one phase of an endless loop: the endorphins feel good, but the thirst always returns.

For many people, this behaviour can feel all but impossible to break because it involves asking oneself, "If I can't get love from others, where will my love come from?". When I considered this question, I realised that to be completely self-sustainable, I had to draw love and connection from deep within me.

Love thyself, to thine self be true.

Your journey of self-love will take time. It won't happen overnight. But it is one of the key ingredients to building Stone Heart. Seek love from the well deep within you, not from others. When you have access to your own well, you become limitless. You are free from the judgments of others and you are free from attachment to dogmas and stories.

I love myself.
I love what I have to offer.
I appreciate myself.

Seeking the validation and approval of others is like saying, "I need someone else's permission to do what I want to do". This suggests that you hold the judgments of others in higher regard than your own self-assessment.

Let me share with you a real example of how I have been challenged by the judgment of others and what I have learned about staying true to my authentic self.

In my personal life, I am reasonably vocal about my spiritual practices. I don't hide them from the world. Further, I don't need the world's approval or acceptance of what I am or what I do. At work, on the other hand, spilling my spiritual practices onto others could be offensive or promote non-inclusivity, so I am careful about how much I share. It's true to my leadership, however, to be outspoken about the laws of the universe and the philosophy of Stone Heart, Light Heart. So when we as a team are confronted by a challenge, I ask my team to first turn in and understand whether there is fear within them that may be manifesting externally as a challenge. We solve business problems by turning in.

Over the years, there have been instances when individuals have passed judgment on my approach to leadership and business management. And it hasn't always been constructive. Some, driven by ego no doubt, have said it's "woo-woo" to turn inward as a first step to business management. When I was a more junior leader, less aware of my own leadership, I often sought the perspective of others to try to find my way to whom I was going to be as an authentic leader. I now realise that I was allowing other people's constructs of leadership to become my own. I was still quite immature in my journey of self-actualisation.

Over the last five years, through failing and learning and failing and learning, I've formed a solid picture of who I am as a leader, irrespective of the judgments of others. My awareness as a leader has been rising and continues to rise. I have learned to be okay with others' judgments and accept that there are many ways to run a company. My way is neither right nor wrong; it's simply my way. Allowing the judgments of others to control me (and my company) did neither me nor my team any favours. So I decided that I would no longer allow my inner truth to be validated or invalidated by anyone else's model of the world.

My organisation, like any other, has seen people come and go. Those who stay practise Stone Heart and live from an empowered base. They don't pass judgment and don't need validation. As a result, we all work in harmony. We are all allowed to express our true nature without fear of what others may say.

TAKING FEEDBACK WITHOUT ACCEPTING JUDGMENT

Being detached from people's judgments and letting go of the need for validation doesn't mean refusing meaningful and constructive feedback. Having the tools to be able to have a challenging conversation, without judgment or ego, in which you can meaningfully contribute to the pool of shared understanding and take feedback in a way that empowers you to grow, is crucial.

In January 2017, a consulting company called Vital Smarts came to the organisation I worked with to teach the company how to have what they branded 'Crucial Conversations'[3]. A Crucial Conversation occurs when the stakes are high and there are opposing opinions and strong emotions. These conversations are tough! They're the ones that make the hairs stand up on the back of your neck.

Let's dissect the three key features of Crucial Conversations as taught by Vital Smarts:

- ❖ **The stakes are high.** There's a burning platform. Between two executives, this might mean that if we can't resolve this conflict, someone's leaving. In an operating theatre, it means our patient could die. (Actually, Crucial Conversations was built for the hospital system!)

- ❖ **There are conflicting opinions.** Each person is completely single-minded in their opinion of what needs to happen, and their opinions are in direct opposition.

- ❖ **Emotions are running high.** Each person is attached to their opinion as if it were their identity. Their limbic brains are in overdrive, pumping out an emotional soup, turning them into animals simply acting out the fight/flight/freeze response.

Figure 8.

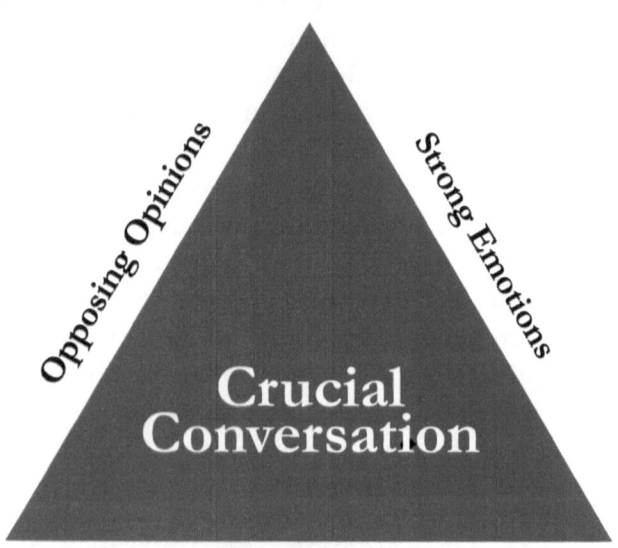

High Stakes

Notice that all sides of the triangle come from the animal mind and egoic thinking. The limbic state gets the better of everyone sometimes, and it takes great conscious awareness to break out of it.

So why do so many Crucial Conversations go so badly? Why do we end up in angry or upset arguments when we actually just wanted to deal with something important? We have our ego to thank. Vital Smarts explain that we *can* hold a Crucial Conversation without ego, but only in a safe space. If the participants don't feel safe, they will go into a state of violence (fight) or silence (flight, freeze).

The giving and receiving of criticism can trigger a Crucial Conversation. And to get the most out of that conversation, you need to be able to both give and accept feedback without ego. The foundations of the Crucial Conversations method are built on the anatomy and behaviour of the brain. It teaches focused techniques to give and accept feedback with Stone Heart, Light Heart. Reading the *Crucial Conversations* book or taking their course will teach you how to do this in more detail, but we'll look at some basics here.

The question is: how do I take positive/negative/constructive feedback in a situation that may awaken my ego and not my higher awareness? And how do I take feedback that may be positive but judgmental?

How do I accept feedback even if I feel it's a judgment?

Thank the person for the feedback, and have the courage to try it on. Experiment with the feedback. See if it fits you. Pick away at the judgment and see if there's any gold in it. Search for the truth and the lesson in it. Some feedback might be rubbish, but some might hold a glimmer of truth. As adults, we can learn through awareness of our own behaviours. Later on, I will talk about looking in the mirror and seeing the truth.

In one conversation, I was told point blank, "You are not a CEO, Stella, you are merely a Sales Manager"; a bold statement from one of the executives in the business I run. I wasn't really prepared for a deep and meaningful conversation, especially one where I was being told that I am not what I quite frankly am. My animal response could have been violent. It could have severed our trust and relationship. I could have dismissed his judgments and continued to dismiss him as time went on.

Instead, after a moment of egoic emotional hurt, I thanked him for his feedback. I took his feedback home and I tried it on. I reflected on how I may be serving as a sales manager rather than a CEO. I gathered new perspectives and learnings. A few weeks later, I thanked my exec for the feedback, as it was valuable in helping me to evolve as a CEO.

The skill here is not to pass judgment on people's judgments of you. Search for any truth, take that truth, and chuck the rest out. Don't let it remain in your energetic sphere. If I'd allowed my exec's judgment to remain in my energetic sphere, he might have taken my place as CEO by now. Life is a series of choices. Don't let your egoic animal brain make them for you.

Stone Heart, Light Heart in Action

Reflect on your current attachments. List ideas that you have a fixed perspective on. Which values do these align to? Do these fixed ideas serve you?

. . . .
. . . .
. . . .
. . . .
. . . .

Reflect on times where you have behaved in ways to gain attention, love, or acceptance from others. What are your typical behaviours? Are you in a behaviour 'loop'? What do you gain when you behave this way?

. . . .
. . . .
. . . .
. . . .
. . . .

Reflect on the past and how you have judged others. What are your typical judgments? What fixed ideas do you have? Do these judgments serve you?

. . . .
. . . .
. . . .
. . . .
. . . .

Upon completing this reflection, what "Aha!"s have surfaced? Have you identified any patterns of behaviour in yourself? Is there anything you wish to stop or change?

. . . .
. . . .
. . . .
. . . .
. . . .

"You can't create a new future holding on to the emotions of the past."

Dr. Joe Dispenza

Chapter 3

Strengthening Stone Heart

"Success is not final, failure is not fatal: it is the courage to continue that counts."

Winston Churchill

What Is Strengthening Stone Heart?

To strengthen a muscle, you go to the gym and you pump iron. This tears fibres in your muscle, stimulating the body to help it heal stronger than before. The more often you repeat this process, the stronger you become. You can strengthen your mind in a similar way. Strengthening your mind is about building frameworks and conditioning around a certain way of thinking. To build that conditioning around Stone Heart, we must nourish and consolidate all of the concepts we covered in Chapters One and Two, including detachment from ego and judgment.

The best opportunity we have to work on our capacity for detachment is in the face of challenges. Challenges are a vehicle for self-reflection, understanding and connection… and they often involve failure. Strengthening Stone Heart is essentially about failing forward. We need to be able to accept failure and make it our friend. Failure is not just something to tolerate; it's something to embrace! If we practise Stone Heart over and over, if we can keep on stuffing up and being okay with it, we can develop strong detachment.

Oftentimes, we see words like 'resilience', 'agility', and 'mental toughness' used as buzzwords, which takes away from their substance and leaves us wondering what they actually mean. So let's be clear right now on what mental toughness is actually all about. Mental toughness is the inner strength and perseverance necessary to detach from your ego. When your ego tells you that you're not good enough, or that you stuffed up, or that you displeased someone, mental toughness is what enables you to detach from that voice, forgive yourself, and keep moving forward.

To strengthen Stone Heart, you must celebrate your failures. To strengthen Stone Heart, you must make failure your good friend. You must embrace failure, recognising that it empowers you to grow and provides the opportunity for new understanding. You can't grow and learn about yourself if you only ever succeed. Muscle rips at the point of failure, and until it does, it will never have the chance to heal stronger.

The central tenet of strengthening Stone Heart is loving the *I* within, and learning how to grow from your inevitable failures is a key part of that. Until you embrace failure, each new failure will prompt another judgment on your sense of self, distancing you from Stone Heart all over again. The more you accept and embrace failure, the more value you will get out of your new awareness of Stone Heart. When you have fully embraced Stone Heart, you will be bolstered by every experience you have, because you can seek the lessons without wasting energy hating yourself for dropping the ball.

WHY IS STRENGTHENING STONE HEART SO IMPORTANT?

Strengthening Stone Heart is important because self-mastery can only be achieved with repetition. There may come a moment in time where you feel you've mastered Stone Heart and you've mastered your ego, but that doesn't mean you won't then spend the next two weeks completely attached to your thoughts. Self-mastery is never permanent; it always needs work.

Strengthening Stone Heart means increasing our detachment from ego by learning from our failures. It enables us to move away from poor self-control and towards self-mastery, and to widen the gap in between so that we are less likely to relapse.

The only thing you can truly control in this world is yourself – but to do that takes consistent, continuous strength.

Strengthen Stone Heart by Embracing the Law of Failure

I first considered my relationship with failure at the age of 36. I was sitting at home after another big flop, feeling pretty deflated. I had employed a seasoned executive recruiter to join our organisation as a director, with the intention of making him a business partner within a year. After 12 months, the time was right to offer him partnership. But he declined the offer, totally blindsiding us. He was off to start his own agency.

If you don't understand the gravity of that, imagine dating someone for a year and being totally in love, living together and planning your shared future. You buy a ring and prepare yourself for that big day where you get to pop the question. You're elated by the thought of spending the rest of your life with them. The day comes, you ask them to marry you, and they say… "No thanks, I'm actually off to marry someone else".

So I sat there that morning in my lounge room, wallowing in failure, and asking myself:

- ❖ What the hell did I do or say that caused this to happen?
- ❖ How am I going to break this to our team? They love him!
- ❖ What does our road to recovery look like?
- ❖ Will we lose business?
- ❖ Will we lose staff?
- ❖ Will we be okay?

❖ But why! We had a deal, why did he change his mind?

❖ Why didn't I see this coming?

I have so many of these stories. If I told them all you'd deflate just listening! In that moment, at 36 years old, I realised that in truth, my life was one big series of failures. But where would I have been without those failures? Could it be that it was the consistency of those failures, the experience of so many great challenges, that ultimately allowed me to learn and grow?

Sure enough, I realised that along with every failure I could recall came a lesson and personal growth. My failures have been my teachers, and I have earned a PhD in life. I've been self-employed since my mid-twenties. With only my friend Failure as my teacher, I've been able to learn business and management.

As I began to realise the truth of failure and its effect on our growth, I felt a great weight lift from me, and I began to weep. No one had ever taught me that it's okay to fail. No one had ever congratulated me for f#*king up or making a mess. And I guess that's not surprising. No one likes to be hurt, and some of my failures have certainly hurt people. As I looked back on my life, I realised that I'd never had a cuddle or received love when I had failed. Failure is dark and lonely. Plus, when you are the leader of a large team, your failures are magnified, impacting not just you but also the people in your tribe – people you love.

But the fact is, in order to grow, one must face failure. Thomas Edison tried 5000 filaments before he found the right one for his electric light bulb. He had a friend in failure. Children fall over and get back up multiple times before mastering their first steps. They too have a friend in failure.

Our very species wouldn't be here without the incalculable failures of our less-evolved selves. The human race has a friend in failure.

Of course, many happy accidents are born from failure, too. If it weren't for the accidental contamination of Alexander Fleming's petri dishes with mould, penicillin may never have been discovered.

This is the law of failure. It's how we test, fail, learn, and grow.

And so I began to embrace failure, finally recognising it as my friend. It had always been there to teach and help me, enabling me to grow with every challenge. I just hadn't seen it until now.

Failure is my friend.

Failure after failure

To say I had a series of career failures before I found recruitment is possibly a bit of an understatement!

I started out in medical school, where I won the Faculty of Health University Medal. You'd be forgiven for thinking I'd have had a stellar career with the hospital, but the reality was quite the opposite: I dropped out after my intern year. It turned out I hated it!

So in 2002, with zero understanding of what it might entail, I opened my first business, Mind Connection, a cognitive therapy practice where I helped people to reprogram their minds. I loved it, but it made no money. I worked my socks off to keep the failing NLP practice running, making everyone I met a patient and charging $180 a session for my inexperience. I spent my Tuesday nights holding the space for a networking group I'd started called Stellarvision. We'd sit in my office burning ylang ylang candles and discussing empowerment and how to change the world. That whole period of my life was wonderful, and I contributed to my community in many ways... but I realise now that I had no idea what I was doing. I was a true novice who thought she was a master.

At this point my finances were going down the pan. I was subsisting on a diet of bread and eggs, and I still couldn't afford my rent. So what did I do? I started a second business! I joined forces with a friend to start a seminar company called Dynamic Conversations. We ran three workshops with 15 people each, and the course was actually really great. But this, too, made no money! By now I'd churned through the whole $30,000 my parents had set aside for me to buy my first house. They'd been saving that money my entire life; I blew it in 12 months.

So, before I could lose any more money, I broke my lease and got my first corporate job, joining Johnson & Johnson as a medical rep. I performed well, and it gave me a chance to recover from the financial mess I had created for myself. They gave me a company car, so I sold mine. I gradually started clawing back some money, and it wasn't long before I was back on my feet. However, it was clear that I didn't fit the corporate mould. I was a rebel and they didn't like it – so eventually I left.

Next, I discovered recruitment. And I was good at it! I found that I could use what I had learned around empathy and relationship management from my cognitive therapy practice. With my entrepreneurial and hustling skills, I built a recruitment desk from scratch. My passion for helping people shone through, and within 12 months I was their leading Asia-Pacific recruiter. Unfortunately, that ended up being a flop too, because the people I worked with had different values to me. Things like porn in the office created an environment where I felt unsafe, and where I couldn't be in alignment with my own values.

I'd been a top performer at everything I'd tried my hand at, but I still hadn't found my fit. I was 26, and unemployed again. No money, again. Flip, flop, flip, flop.

I understand now that the flip-flopping was an important, if tedious, part of the journey to my current destination. It helped to shape both my head and my heart, providing clarity and definition around what I wanted to do with my days.

I started my organisation, Reo Group, in 2009. I was a rookie with only two years' experience in the game, and the next ten years were a rocky journey of learning how to be a CEO. Running Reo Group has been my biggest challenge. As a start-up in a saturated market post–global financial crisis, Reo Group has presented challenge after exhausting challenge. But these relentless challenges were exactly what I needed. I have my dear friend Failure at The School of Hard Knocks to thank for teaching me the skills I needed to be a great CEO.

Riding the waves of failure

Life's a beach, and the waves never stop coming. There is never a moment when the moon stops pulling and the sea stays still. As long as you keep swimming in the waves of life, you'll keep facing new challenges.

But you might just get better at conquering them.

Maybe you get dunked by the first wave, getting sand in your undies and your ears. Embarrassed as you are, you resurface, ready to take on another. The second wave fills your nose with water. But you're ready to face a third. With every wave, you are better prepared for the next. You learn that you can either swim under or over them. The further out you go, the more strength and skill you need.

Eventually, you learn to use a board to surf in and out. Now you begin to grow your skills further, learning how to ride and conquer these waves. And once you become adept at surfing, being dunked feels like no more than a distant memory.

I am a surfer of many waves: the waves of my marriage, my business, my kids, my health. I have learned to ride the waves of my life. The more I ride, the easier it feels. Now, even the biggest waves feel like mere ripples. I'm not scared of the waves anymore; I welcome them. Big ones can be a lot of fun! I'm not afraid of falling off, because I know how to swim and how to climb back on. And I appreciate the opportunity to learn from my mistakes. I welcome failure, because every time I fail, I grow.

LEARNING TO RECOVER FROM FAILURE

None of this is to say that failure doesn't still hurt. It does! Mainly your ego! That's why strengthening Stone Heart is a key part of building a friendship with failure, and vice versa. To welcome failure in your life, you need to learn how to detach from the hurt your ego may feel and lead your own recovery from failure.

The cycle of growth is exactly that – a cycle. You need to work until you fail, then stop, learn, and recover, similar to the cycle the body goes through to grow new muscle fibres. Then, with your new learnings, you go back out and do it all again. It might hurt sometimes, but that's okay, because you know that this is the path to true growth.

Your ability to recover from failure is critical to strengthening your Stone Heart. The stronger your Stone Heart, the quicker you recover from failure – but the reverse is true, too. It's a positive feedback loop: each time you learn and grow from failure, you put yourself in a stronger position to recover from the next failure. The quicker you recover, the sooner you're back on your feet and growing again. And the more times you complete the loop, the more you start to create a positive rather than a negative association with failure. That's why resilient people tend to achieve what they desire in life. They have mastered the fail-recover-grow feedback loop.

Recovery requires time, energy, and space to grow. It took me just over a year to recover from my business failure at Mind Connection, and it was the time I spent at J&J that gave me the space to do that. Recovery from failure is an important step in the cycle of growth. It gives you room to absorb and integrate your new learnings, which is necessary for growth.

Accepting the cycle of growth will help you to cultivate a friendship with failure. As you do, your appetite for risk will increase. You will have more energy and excitement to try new things. You will have more confidence to throw yourself into new activities. Consequently, you will fail a lot more! And as you now know, that's a good thing! Strengthening Stone Heart is about practising the cycle of growth and living by the law of failure, without judgment of yourself or others. This builds your mental toughness and thickens your skin.

I firmly believe that nothing can cut through my (metaphorical!) skin. Each failure is just that. It isn't the end, and it doesn't have to be painful. I don't have a strong association of pain with failure like many of us do. We are conditioned to associate pain with failure, but this is incredibly un-serving for us all. Through NLP practices, I have rewired my mind so that failure equals growth and pleasure, not pain.

That's the rewiring that I am asking you to consider for yourself. Shift gears.

Reflect now on your personal association with failure. When you fail, how much does it hurt? Do you think you could rewire your relationship with failure? Could it be more pleasurable? I know I'm asking you to consider a framework of thinking that is a 180-degree reversal of what you've been taught, but as the saying goes, if you keep doing what you've always done, you'll keep getting what you've always got.

To recover from failure is to bounce.

Bounce

To bounce is to rebound. When a ball falls, it bounces and comes back up. Of course, how high it bounces depends on what sort of stuff it's made of!

Your ability to bounce is based on your personal belief system around learning. We all have choices. You can be a medicine ball that accelerates down to the ground and lands with a thud. Or you can be a basketball, accelerating to the ground and bouncing back just as fast.

Strengthening Stone Heart helps you to bounce higher after you fall.

Stone Heart is strong because it approaches problems and challenges in life with the right frame of mind. Stone Heart wastes no time between challenges. Stone Heart bounces back quickly and often.

When I was 19, my mum said to me, "Stella, you have a cold heart, there's ice in there!" I can't remember the exact context, but she was upset and I was detached – and that detachment came off as coldness. But it wasn't that I didn't care; it was just that I didn't let it affect the way I felt.

Stone Heart enables you to control your emotions, putting you in charge rather than the animals at the zoo. There is great power in being non-emotional in response to events. In the second section of this book, you will learn that non-emotionality doesn't mean you don't love or experience great joy; it just means you don't live at the mercy of the zoo. You can *choose* the emotions you feel.

My mum's description of my heart is where the very phrase Stone Heart comes from. Thanks Mum!

BOUNCE TO A BETTER YOU

When Jack Welch launched the GE x10 framework in the mid-eighties, he said, "I would love to have a management team that really understood the CVS x10 = BVS equation. It's the value-added role in the management process".

GE x10 thinking is an approach to growth designed by Michael Hewitt-Gleeson[4] especially for Jack Welch and GE, and its central principle is the CVS to BVS equation. This beautifully simple but immensely powerful equation describes a constant cycle of growth and is a great framework for solving problems.[5]

When Welch launched the x10 framework, GE was worth USD 35 billion. By the time he left in 2001, that had risen to USD 484 billion, making it the world's most valuable company. Suffice to say the x10 framework is an effective formula for growth!

Let's take a closer look at what I call the 'growth equation'.

CVS (current view state) x *10 = BVS (better view state)*

So what does this actually mean?

Well, if I take my current state and multiply it by 10, this is what my future state could look like. X10 thinking is basically about recognising the immense capacity we have for growth – it is always possible to envisage and work towards a better view state that is a full ten times better than our current state.

X10 thinking gives us a framework to solve problems by exploring what our BVS could look like. What would a better view or a better version look like? Can you find one that is ten times better than your current state? This approach encourages you to engage your creative centres, to take the time and space to envisage a powerfully bright future. Some of the best creations and solutions to problems have been achieved using this framework of thinking.

When I reflect on the tenets of good leadership and how we as individuals build good leadership, I believe one of the most important aspects is regularly applying the CVS to BVS equation on yourself. Looking in the mirror and asking yourself what your BVS looks like not so much physically, but mentally and emotionally. This framework of thinking strengthens Stone Heart. It gives you a way of being that says, "Even if where I am isn't optimal, I know I can move to a better place".

Let's say you just royally stuffed something up. Oops. Something is now broken, or you have hurt someone by saying something silly. What do you do?

Apply the equation.

Start with CVS = your current situation.

Next, consider all possible scenarios that would be better than your current situation. This is where you apply the CVS to BVS equation. Consider your CVS and ideate new options for yourself that are ten times better. Do this again and again, until you find the one that resonates. Now you have a new BVS to work towards.

With time (and effort!), this BVS becomes your new CVS.

And that's growth.

Forgiveness

One of the secret ingredients to getting the most out of the growth equation is forgiveness. This means both forgiveness of self and forgiveness of others. In a sense, forgiveness is just another word for detachment. Detachment from self, detachment from self-perception, detachment from the results you create. Only through detachment from judgment can one truly experience connection to self and the love for self that can be nurtured deep within. You've just got to be able to forgive yourself.

Many people don't understand what forgiveness is, or how to forgive. Part of the reason they find it so hard is that they don't realise that forgiveness is just a form of detachment. To forgive someone, something, or yourself, you have to be able to detach from every element of that moment. Detachment is how you begin the journey of forgiveness. And forgiveness is the key to recovery.

I was in my thirties when I started berating myself. At the time, I was the go-to person for my 15 members of staff, not to mention my two children. After suffering through multiple crises, both personal and professional, with very little support, I found myself on the slippery slope of self-hatred. Around the same time, I began to feel pain in my left breast and took myself in for a mammogram. I received the all-clear, but my doctor told me, "Stella, you are under too much stress, you need to remove some stressors from your life."

The negative energy around me had made its way into my body, manifesting itself as aches and pains – my body's way of trying to make me stop and look in the mirror. Had I not made the necessary changes, I've no doubt that energy would ultimately have manifested a disease of some sort. Weak and demoralised, I felt unable to face even one more challenge – but of course, more came. In the following days, my two-year-old caught hand, foot and mouth disease; my four-year-old got a UTI; and I got a speeding fine.

Of course, my speeding fine was simply a symptom. Marginal speeding is a sign that you are not present, floating along, reacting rather than deciding. Although really, I didn't need a speeding ticket to tell me that I felt like a zombie! I was dividing my energy between a million different areas of my life, and failing at everything. During this time, not much was in flow. Business was suffering. Results were average. The leadership team weren't connected and harmonised to work to one vision. I really felt like I was failing.

And so began the relapse of negative self-talk, monkey mind activity, and a downward spiral in my mental and spiritual energy. I was in a dangerous place. I remember it as a moment in my life where I had a lot of self-hate. Self-deprivation. I began to say some horrible things to myself, like "You are a failure. You are not worthy of success. You are not a good leader. People don't respect you. You won't make it."

Then, in June 2017, I learned how to love and forgive myself.

Since 2016, I had been working closely with a shaman from Chile. She has been my greatest teacher, and I continue to visit her every couple of months. When I went to visit her that June, I was carrying a load of baggage from a difficult month. Before I had even mentioned it, she noticed my low energetic state and asked me to recite an affirmation.

> *I appreciate my commitment to want to be better.*
> *I appreciate my love for myself and others.*
> *I appreciate the joy from my learnings.*
> *I appreciate the gateways of opportunities.*
> *I appreciate I can hear the truth.*

STONE HEART, LIGHT HEART

I appreciate I can slow down and go somewhere else.
I appreciate the tribes that help me.
I appreciate the life I've created and manifested.
I appreciate the love of my family.
I appreciate the stillness.

I immediately began to open up and feel lighter. The affirmation shifted my judgment of what was happening, and I began to appreciate the moment I was experiencing.

To reconnect with myself, I began to write down what I appreciated in myself. As I did, I realised that before that moment, much of my language about life and self had been very damaging. I'd engaged in a lot of self-deprivation and self-blame, and experienced frequent feelings of worthlessness – all of which came down to judgment of self. That wasn't me. I am – as are you – an infinite being, a transporter of light, an intelligent, loving consciousness with the power to manifest and materialise all that I want in life. (Obviously this doesn't mean "I think about a Ferrari, therefore I create a Ferrari" – you and I both know that desire comes from ego, not consciousness.)

Releasing all these negative thought patterns through self-love proclamations and affirmations shifted my thinking and helped me detach, and immediately I began to see a corresponding change in the world around me.

What had changed? My inner language.

I realised that we co-create our reality with the words we think and say. The energy we give out drives and creates our material universe. The outer world is a reflection of the inner world: on some level, everything we think and say is mirrored back. So when your outer world is spinning out of control, don't battle with it. Instead, stop and assess your inner world. This is where the change needs to be made.

There is power in stillness, as it gives you a pause to turn inward. When you do stop and turn in, you will likely find the triggers for your low energetic state. And herein lies the key to forgiveness. These triggers are the very things that you will need to detach from in order to forgive. Forgiveness starts with realising that the foundation of forgiveness is detachment. And it continues with finding out what you need to detach from.

Self-forgiveness is the release of a value judgment we have placed upon ourselves. For me to forgive myself, I have to release my judgments of myself and realise that my mistakes, my hurt, my vengeance are all opportunities for turning inward, learning about myself, and growing as a person. The greatest gift is to know thyself. Forgiveness or detachment from self and self-judgment is the gateway to experiencing this.

Similarly, forgiving others is also about letting go of a value judgment. If I forgive you, it means that I am no longer judging what you did as hurtful to me. And for me to let go of that judgment, I must first detach from that hurt. Only when you achieve true forgiveness through absolute detachment can you really be complete and find peace.

The journey of self-forgiveness can start with an affirmation similar to the one I used. Affirmation is a self-soothing technique that can be used to shift gears from hating to loving. Whenever I hear self-judgments come forward in my consciousness, I stop, be still, and affirm to myself what I appreciate. In that way, I allow my thoughts to co-create the things I want, not the things I don't want. Real forgiveness comes from realising that there is nothing to forgive. Everything is in divine order for you. All you need to do is stop the judgment, and Stone Heart will awaken.

Learning how to forgive yourself is part of the journey of strengthening Stone Heart. It's key to recovering quickly after challenge or failure so that you can continue to move through the cycle of learning and growth.

WHEN LIFE KEEPS REPEATING THE SAME CHALLENGE

I believe everyone has a personal purpose for existing in this world. Paulo Coelho, author of *The Alchemist,* calls this your 'personal legend'. We will cover this when we learn about Light Heart. Depending on your personal purpose and where you are in relation to living out your purpose, you can often predict your discords and challenges. I am a firm believer that the universe will issue you the same challenge over and over until you actually learn from it. There is wisdom to be found in every event, every experience. But we don't always see it. Take the analogy of a video game. A video game has certain levels, and at each level you need to conquer different obstacles to get to the next level. Until such stage that you can conquer the game. Sometimes you have to repeat the same level over and over again, until you can master the tricky bits that get you through the hoop. The mastery of that particular hoop is what allows you to reach the end of the level. Life's challenges operate in similar ways. You'll keep getting issued the same challenge until you can master it.

I have seen this many times in women who attract (and are attracted to) the wrong men. I knew a young woman who, in her heart, wanted a loving and faithful family man, but every man she dated just wanted sex. When she spoke about it, her language gave away her monkey mind's fantasies about wild sex with Brad Pitt lookalikes. Her behaviour was being driven by unconscious desires based in her reptilian brain. If she genuinely wanted to find a loving long-term partner, she needed to turn in and reprogram those unconscious patterns. By reflecting at a conscious level, she could expect her unconscious thinking patterns about men and sex to change accordingly.

We attract that which we unconsciously believe. What we believe and think repeatedly is in connection with our purpose. If there is a repeated challenge, failure or discord that you keep facing, take stock and turn inward to uncover the mental patterns that are running your life – and then work to change them.

When we all realise that we are, in fact, in control of our own minds, we uncover the power to change our unconscious patterns, too. We become the curator of our desires and therefore our destiny. This is the task of Stone Heart, learning how to unpick your unconscious patterns.

I believe reality is created first in the mind of the viewer – and the viewer of your destiny is you. If you don't like what you see, change it on the inside, and the outside will follow.

How to Use Your Courage

Playing life at 100% and embracing failure takes courage.

To be a leader, one must have the courage to look inward. Learning about your personal leadership will require you to draw deeply from your courage reserves. When I was in my twenties, I had enough courage that I could have spared some to sell on eBay! As I grew older and I started to learn about personal leadership, however, I began to lose my courage. And the very fact that I was losing courage dampened my confidence further. After all, how can you lead if you have no courage?

So where had my courage gone? And more importantly, *why* had it gone?

The business landscape suffers no fools. You are only as good as your last transaction, and everything you do and say is susceptible to scrutiny, judgment, opinion, and analysis. You can't hide; you're constantly being assessed on all fronts. The stakes are high. One wrong move, one wrong word could lead to big losses and serious failure. For me, this pressure was a poison, slowly eroding my courage.

Personal leadership is tough to learn, because it takes failure, feedback, reflection, and time to implement new behaviours. It takes humility, and consistent receptivity to constructive feedback. In an effort to be the best possible leader, I had opened myself up to feedback and the guidance of those wiser than me. But accepting feedback to better yourself, as valuable as it may be, can also be soul-crushing – and it can take time to re-establish your confidence.

I was quite vulnerable during this period of growth. I felt emotionally exposed. My decisions lacked certainty and I was tentative about making bold or risky moves. I went from playing a big game and crushing it to playing a small game with no big risks and no big rewards.

I'd better not say that, it might hurt someone.
I'd better not do that, it might put people off.
I'd better not make that decision, I'll wait for someone else to do it.

In my desire for perfection and success, I lost my courage to do what it takes to actually achieve great success. Chasing the perfect decisions, to get the perfect results, to be the perfect leader… it's exhausting! Worse, it's counterproductive.

I now know that being a great leader is about going all out even if you have no idea what you are doing. Sometimes (most times!), I have no idea what I'm doing. I am a seasoned head-hunter but a novice CEO. I'm learning as I go. As my experience grows, so does my ability to make good decisions without hesitation. But to acquire experience is to suck it and see. I needed to play as big as I could, while remaining caring and heart-centred.

Having courage is about jumping into the arena even if you know you're not going to win. Choosing bold and risky moves, showing emotion and going for what you want even if you know you are going to (temporarily) suck at it. Courage means telling that special someone how you feel; asking for that promotion; giving that uncomfortable but constructive criticism. When you stop trying for fear of failing, you slowly poison your courage.

What would happen if you were to just play big, even when the stakes were high, and accept failure as a possible outcome?

I talk a lot about building your inner strength so you don't need validation from the outside world. The courage to act doesn't require external validation. Self-assured people don't need their actions to be validated by others.

When faced with a challenge, call on your courage. Give it a go. Don't take feedback and opinions from people who aren't playing in the arena with you. It's easy to point fingers, throw judgment, and criticise from the stands. The spectators' commentary must be silenced. In this silence, your courage will have the space to thrive.

Choose to play life at 100% and accept the spectrum of potential outcomes, from nailing it to failing it.

Stone Heart, Light Heart in Action

Write down a list of traits and behaviours present in your current view state (CVS) of a particular aspect of your life (perhaps as a leader, an athlete, or a parent). For each item, ask yourself how these traits or behaviours could change to create a better view state (BVS).

Some views won't change, because you are already operating optimally. But x10 thinking holds that, overall, you should be able to achieve a BVS that's ten times better than your CVS.

Looking at your BVS, which behaviours/habits/ways of thinking stand out as things that you can change immediately? Circle or highlight these.

CVS	BVS (CVS x10)
....	....
....	....
....	....
....	....
....	....
....	....
....	....
....	....
....	....
....	....

Are you a medicine ball or a basketball? How high do you bounce?

Draw two columns. In the first, write down any judgments or baggage you might be holding on to that may be preventing you from bouncing as well as you otherwise could. In the second column, write down the learnings you can take away from that.

Judgments	**Learnings**
. . . .	. . . .
. . . .	. . . .
. . . .	. . . .
. . . .	. . . .
. . . .	. . . .
. . . .	. . . .
. . . .	. . . .
. . . .	. . . .
. . . .	. . . .
. . . .	. . . .
. . . .	. . . .
. . . .	. . . .
. . . .	. . . .
. . . .	. . . .
. . . .	. . . .

Your word is your wand. What you say repeatedly becomes your reality.

CHAPTER 4

ACCELERATING STONE HEART

"Words are the vibrations of nature. Beautiful words create beautiful nature; ugly words create ugly nature. This is the root of the universe."

Dr Masaru Emoto

What Is Accelerating Stone Heart?

I hope that Stone Heart is resonating with you and you have started building a strong foundation to awaken and strengthen Stone Heart by integrating the concepts we have covered so far. The next step is to accelerate that aspect within you. Awakening Stone Heart starts with understanding the canvas of your mind. It sheds light on your unconscious patterns of thinking and challenges you to ask, "Who is in control, me or the zoo?". This awakening grows as you begin to think about things in a new way, and strengthens as you embrace failure and learn to love the *I* within.

Now it's time to accelerate your awakening. In this chapter you will learn to empower this aspect of yourself so that it becomes more prominent and consistent in your life.

Why is accelerating Stone Heart so important?

Accelerating Stone Heart is about deepening self-control and increasing consistency.

Consistency means interacting with the world in a logical, self-driven way. If we're caught up in ego, our reactions will fluctuate wildly depending on our feelings in the moment and our judgments of the actions of others. If instead we allow our reactions to be driven by our true self rather than by the layers around us, we can build consistency in our behaviours. Accelerating Stone Heart helps us to do this.

Self-control involves mastering the layers of your ego (and there are many!). These layers might be the way you view yourself, the way you view others, all of the filters of your judgements, and all of the filters of your belief systems. When we master one layer, oftentimes we expose another. When we accelerate Stone Heart, we accelerate this process towards self-mastery. The higher pace is going to take some getting used to. Where it once may have taken you a week or two to realise you were casting judgment, ultimately you will find it takes an instant.

Every human can master their mind. Let's talk about how you can increase the velocity with which you can return home to yourself.

Strengthening Stone Heart means spending more time connected with it. Accelerating Stone Heart means increasing the speed and depth with which you connect. You get deeper into your sense of self as you master each of your values and change your belief systems accordingly. With each new learning comes the opportunity to overcome a new challenge.

Mastering yourself is a journey with no true destination. It's a journey of turning in. The very idea of a destination is ego driven. Having a destination suggests that there is a right place to finish. And when we choose a right place to finish, what are we doing? We're making a judgment, the very thing we're learning to avoid!

Other people need to know this, too. How many suffer with mental illness that gets blamed on their brain, as if it's something they have zero control over? This devolution of power does them a great disservice. We have more control than we think.

Accelerate Stone Heart by Creating Your Own Reality

Sometimes, life's chaos manages to wiggle its way into your internal world, making it hard to keep tabs on the truth. The easiest way to break that pattern and come back into your power is to look in the mirror.

Looking in the mirror is a metaphor for looking within yourself. When you look in the mirror, what do you see? What do you hear? What's the voice in your head saying?

When I first met my husband, I had just turned 24. I met him at a seminar. At the time, I was having a fling with the curator and word got around. On our first date, my future husband asked me point blank about the veracity of the rumours. I denied it, of course. As if I was going to tell the truth; I'd only just met the guy! Who asks that on a first date, anyway?

Two years and one marriage later, we were living in an apartment in Sydney. I was suffering terribly from a gynaecological condition called cervical intraepithelial neoplasia (CIN), which can lead to cervical cancer. My NLP training had taught me that every disease is a symptom of the mind manifested in the body, so I was really troubled as to why I had this awful disease. I wasn't aware of any issues or triggers that might have caused this.

My training had also taught me that by looking in the mirror, you can identify the source of a symptom. So one Thursday night, I sat on my bed, closed my eyes, and went inward. I ran a series of 'home truth' tests on myself to try to work out why the hell I had manifested stage-four CIN. What was in it, and what had created it?

While in deep meditation, I heard a voice say, "You are a liar". I followed that thread, and was able to recognise the source of my trouble: I had been holding on to the lie I'd told my husband on our very first date. The lie about my fling had manifested as cervical disease, I felt sure of it. And I felt equally sure there was no way I would have consciously been able to comprehend that without deliberately looking in the mirror to seek the truth.

If I hadn't had the courage to recognise and accept my ugly truth and tell my husband about my lie, I couldn't have healed. The CIN might well have progressed to cervical cancer. Confessing was a challenge; I knew that it could destroy the trust in our relationship. But not confessing, I could now see, wasn't an option.

I told him how I'd lied to him, and that I believed my lie had manifested itself as CIN. I explained that I needed to tell him the truth so that I could heal.

The truth will set you free.

He walked out on me that night. He just grabbed the car keys and walked out, leaving me with a boatload of unanswered questions: Would he come back? Would he still love me? Was this the end?

I sat there in my truth with so much sadness. I'd accepted a sacrifice: the love of my life in return for my physical health and healing. You can't own your body unless you own the truths that are running it. At the end of the day, I was at peace with my decision. I was free. My healing had begun, and I was willing to accept the consequences, whatever they may be.

My husband came home that night.

When he walked through the door, I was sobbing. I asked him for his understanding. He hugged me and told me that he loved me.

I haven't had a cervical issue since that day, and I am confident I won't ever have cervical issues again.

Learn to lean into the truth. Look in the mirror. Strengthen your resolve. Don't look for the beauty; look for the truth. Many people struggle to do this, worried they will loathe what they see. But seeking your truth can wake you up to a new beauty within.

Your Word is Your Wand

You know by now that your thoughts become your reality – and that includes the language you use. That which you repeat is that which you become. Your inner monologue, whether it be the voice of your monkey mind or the voice of your inner wisdom, translates to your external reality.

Your word is your wand. You actualise the words that you repeat to yourself and others. This means you wield enormous power over your own reality.

Reflect on the words you say to yourself when no one is listening. Do these words serve you or bring you down?

Reflect on the words you say about others. Do these words serve you or bring you down?

Reflect on the words you use in your leadership. How do you talk to your colleagues, your staff, your manager? Do these words serve you or bring you down?

We talk our way into different circumstances all day long. The way we communicate with ourselves and others becomes the highway to our immediate future. Your reality is a continuous creation, designed by you and forged with the words you use and listen to.

Don't let your monkey mind trick you into thinking that this is hocus-pocus. Perhaps you've been wishing for a new Ferrari, yet your Nissan Pulsar still sits stubbornly in the driveway. Your mind will bring up examples like this, attempting to debunk the theory, all the while reining in your power. But manifestation is not about actualising desires driven by the ego. Manifestation only works when you connect with your true self to understand and put into words what it is you really want at a deeper level.

In Chapter Two, we examined the NLP communication model. We discovered how an external event passes through your internal filters to give you a state, which in turn causes an emotional reaction in the monkey mind, which then impacts your behaviour.

How you act (what you say and do) is then met externally with an equal and opposite reaction, continuing the cycle of cause and effect. Your words are a part of this cycle. Your inner state can often dictate the things you say to yourself and others.

Energy is not invisible; it can be measured and mastered. And the first stage of energetic channelling that must be consciously mastered is sound. Sound waves are the primary translation of spirit into matter. The energy of a sound wave is the first perceptible stage of physical manifestation of thought. When we recognise this transformation of energy, we become stronger in our ability to translate thought into sound. The stronger our energetic practice becomes, the more effectively we can manifest and materialise our desires.

I am a student of this wisdom. I have dedicated hours and hours of meditation to it, across many years of my life. I can think and create very quickly now. Sometimes it looks like magic. I'll tell a co-worker my week's goal of connecting with Joe Bloggs and minutes later, Joe Bloggs will call the office looking for me!

Mastery of materialisation from thought to reality using the power of sound begins with awakening and strengthening Stone Heart. If you cannot detach, if you still judge and feel impacted by judgment, you cannot master this power. With all the criminal activities, violence, and natural disasters that plague the world around us, it can be a challenge to disconnect emotionally. But it can be done. I'm asking you to get off the rollercoaster. The rollercoaster will continue on its path but, with your feet planted firmly on the ground, you can choose the perspective from which you look at it.

When you clear the canvas of your mind of destructive or unserving thoughts, you create space to work with your powers more deeply. So, learn to reframe destructive comments into constructive ones. Refuse gossip. Repeat a simple affirmation to yourself each day.

Affirmations work because they cause your internal state to shift. The wiring of your brain literally transforms, establishing more efficacious neural pathways. Your unconscious behavioural patterns then shift towards these new pathways, effecting more resourceful actions. Affirmations affect your results instantly because they supply your continuously created reality with a new energy.

My daily work on language and thinking is empowered by my meditation practice. I look for limiting thoughts and worthless emotions. If I find them, these little termites eating away at my clean thinking, I immediately exterminate them. I know that if I allow these thoughts to stay, my power to think and create will slow down. These silly little thoughts and emotions are obstacles for my energetic channelling; they don't serve me.

Every time you speak, you are making agreements with people, with the energy around you, and with your own spirit. Being the guardian of your voice, then – your inner voice as well as your outer voice – is the single most important thing.

So how can we become alchemists of our language?

If you are committed to the goal of empowering your spirit and mastering the *I* within, being clean with your thoughts and considerate with your words will become easy. But it won't happen overnight. For me personally, on a spiritual level, it's taken a long time to fully practise what I preach.

Imagine if every time you thought a thought, it instantly materialised. If that were true, we would be much more conscious of our voices. However, since the process is more subtle than that, we don't tend to pay so much attention to the words we use. This is why it takes time and dedication to recognise the connection between your inner world and your outer world, and foster that connection through language. It all starts with Stone Heart.

When we make it a priority to remain detached from the outer world, we can actively finetune our thoughts and emotions to align them with our spirit. The secret is to not let your inner world be lost to your outer world. That is, pay less attention to what's happening around you and more to what's happening inside you. Your energy source is within.

When you nurture that, you accelerate Stone Heart, and you can conquer anything. When you have mastered Stone Heart, you will be able to witness the outer world without losing yourself in its drama.

Mantras

Mantras are an important part of keeping your inner world in alignment with your intention. They help you to reprogram your monkey mind away from limiting self-talk and towards more productive self-talk. I use mantras to exercise my conscious mind in the same way that I go to the gym to exercise my physical body.

Your unconscious mind is an obedient listener to your conscious mind. If your conscious mind is not clear on its intention and articulate in its language, then you're not in control of the narrative you're giving your unconscious mind – which means you're not in control of your reality.

Many people are cynical about mantras. And sure enough, repeating to yourself over and over "I love the gym, I love the gym, I love the gym" will not make you, in that present moment, love the gym! But mantras are not about instant gratification. Rather, repetition of a narrative over time will gradually reprogram your unconscious so that *eventually* that narrative becomes your reality. In this case, you will eventually love the gym!

Here are a few examples of powerful mantras:

My inner world takes precedence over my outer world.

My outer world is taken care of.

I am safe wherever I am.

STONE HEART, LIGHT HEART

I am present.

I give in to this moment.

I am not here to fix things; I am here to create.

I am the alchemist of my life.

I talk in alignment with my consciousness, not my ego.

I am a student of my message.

What I say will be done.

I validate myself.

I use personal mantras, but I also use mantras with my children. When my kids were little, they suffered from nightmares. When I brought my mantra practice into the kids' bedtime routine, it made a remarkable difference to their ability to nod off calmly and sleep through the night. The mantra I use with my kids is unique to their needs.

Our ritual looks like this: Before I tuck my children in, we run through a series of meditations. I rub a floral cologne between my hands and the relaxing scent acts as an anchor to break state and maintain presence. We do a breathing exercise and I repeat the mantra, "I cleanse you of all negative energy".

We also do a chakra-balancing exercise which helps them to relax, teaches them the philosophies of Stone Heart, Light Heart and builds unconscious habits of positive self-talk. This is just one example of how I use Stone Heart, Light Heart in my parenting. It is not enough just to understand this wisdom: I must continually practise it, not just for my own benefit but also for those I love.

I want my kids to grow up with this practice so that as they grow into young adults they already understand the philosophy and power of Stone Heart, Light Heart. This inner power is my biggest gift to them. It gives me so much joy to go for a bushwalk and hear my youngest say, "Mum, there's great energy here, let's meditate" without judgment or the all-too-common preconceived idea that turning inward is difficult or woo-woo.

Practise what you preach.

HABITS = DISCIPLINE + HARD WORK

There's ample evidence to show that discipline and hard work trump talent and ability. Angela Duckworth, psychologist and author of *Grit*, has dedicated her life to understanding what makes people successful[6]. What makes a child become a world-renowned pianist? What takes a uni dropout from failure to prosperity? Study after study has shown that consistent hard work is the greatest predictor of success.[7] Imagine if Federer gave up on practice. Imagine if Mandela gave up on hope. Imagine our world if our innovators, leaders, and creators simply gave up. Where would we be?

I'm not naturally smart. In fact, I think I am an average performer. But throughout my life, I have worked longer, harder, and with more focus than my peers. I've prioritised the skills that matter most to me, and focused my energy on them. This, I believe, is the key to success. The magic is in mastering the mundane.

But how do you actually do that when there are so many plates to spin and challenges to face? How does a new mum look after her baby, get enough sleep, and return to work? How does an executive stay on top of her social life, her accounts, and her laundry? How does a police officer keep his marriage happy, his diet balanced, and his carbon footprint low? The answer: habits.

Habits are misunderstood. They're not just repeating an action or behaviour at the same time each day, in exactly the same way. A true habit, one that contains both discipline and hard work, is the joining of two mantras:

Always do your best.
Be consistent.

The concept of "always do your best" is often misunderstood. In his incredible book *The Four Agreements*, Don Miguel Ruiz talks about how doing your best doesn't look the same in all situations. This is a hugely important realisation to come to. Believing that "your best" equals "the absolute best you can do under the most suitable of circumstances" is a trap which leads to unreasonable expectations and self-judgment. A sprinter can't expect themselves to run a personal best in every single race! Instead, aim to always do your best *relative to what is possible* in your situation.

If you're running your 100-metre sprint into a headwind, your time will look different than it would in optimal conditions. You can still do your best. If you're at home looking after three kids, the amount of paid work you get done will be less than if you've got an uninterrupted day in the office. You can still do your best. Just because the outcome looks different doesn't mean you didn't do your best. Ultimately, it's not about the outcome – it's about knowing you gave it everything you had. This attitude is where the acceleration of your growth comes from.

The concept "be consistent" relates to the discipline of doing something again and again. A habit must necessarily be consistent – otherwise, it's just a one-off effort. The most important thing to remember is that consistency is connected to the *doing* of the habit, not to the time, or place, or some other external factor. Your habit may look surprisingly different from day to day. Consistency demands only that it still be done. For example, perhaps you have a gym habit where you get up early each morning to do a workout. Most mornings you give yourself a good hour to warm up, work out, and pay attention to your body. But suppose one morning you have an important business meeting scheduled partway through your gym time. This doesn't mean you have to break your habit. Being consistent with your habit means keeping that habit in some way, even if the particulars look different. Maybe this morning's gym session is shorter. But you still do it. Maybe today's gym session moves to the afternoon. But you still do it. Either way, your habit has consistency.

True habits are created when you do your best, and do it consistently.

In accelerating Stone Heart, I have come to realise that my success is directly related to the discipline I apply to my habits. I meet many people who place all their focus on their goals and new year's resolutions, but never seem to meet them. Why? Because they're thinking too much about the destination and not enough about the journey.

Your goals are important, but the journey towards them constitutes the majority of your experience and therefore your happiness. If the journey to achieving your goal sucks, the whole experience loses its lustre. Maybe you'll ultimately achieve your goal, but as soon as the goal is won, the party is over and you're back to feeling dissatisfied.

Stone Heart asks you to create daily habits that will help move you towards success and happiness. A goal is something you want to achieve, whereas a habit is a consistent behaviour (no excuses!). It's something you do routinely, usually in pursuit of a goal. Those who have accelerated Stone Heart keep habits that align with their goals.

In year 12, I wanted to get a HSC result in the high nineties. I created a habit for that year of studying from 6-pm to 11-pm on weekdays, and 8-am to noon on Saturdays and Sundays – 33 hours of study per week on top of my school schedule. I didn't miss a day. And I still got to spend my Saturday and Sunday afternoons with my family and my boyfriend. I achieved the result I sought, not thanks to my smarts, but thanks to my habits.

Now, as a businesswoman and a mother of two, I have a few more plates to spin. As adults, we don't have the luxury of such one-dimensional habits; we have to accommodate all areas of life and learn to prioritise based on our values.

My personal habits align with the three core areas of my life: me, family, and work. Everything else in life is not a priority – it's that simple.

My daily habits for myself include meditating, journaling, working out, and reading – these support my spiritual practice and help me stay healthy, both physically and mentally. When it comes to my family, my habits include preparing the kids for school, playing with them when they get back, helping them with their homework, and getting them to bed every night. And I make sure to set aside time to connect with my husband. My weekly work schedule allots time to strategy, business growth, development, numbers, validations, leadership, one-on-ones, etc. This schedule is also a habit.

Each of these habits has a consistent place in my diary. My days and weeks follow a pattern, which means I don't have to think about them – they just happen. It's routine.

Habits take the thinking out of the game.

I can allocate goals and targets within my routine and achieve them all, because my results depend on the framework of my habits – not desire or motivation, which may be at the mercy of my monkey mind and my hormones. I definitely don't rely on my monkey mind to achieve my goals. I detach from the zoo, and I implement habits.

Stone Heart doesn't rely on emotions like desire, drive, or excitement to achieve goals. Stone Heart builds and honours habits, creating space for mastery.

Stone Heart, Light Heart in Action

Write down a mantra that you can say to yourself to build your Stone Heart – a mantra that will help you remain detached from your monkey mind and stay connected to your inner power.

. . . .
. . . .
. . . .
. . . .
. . . .

List all of your values and the areas of life that bring you most joy.

. . . .
. . . .
. . . .
. . . .
. . . .

Now brainstorm some daily/weekly habits that could lead you towards mastery in those areas of life.

....
....
....
....
....

Finally, design a schedule of habits that will support you in your journey towards mastery.

....
....
....
....
....

You are not the centre of the universe.

Chapter 5

Leading with Stone Heart

"Don't ever put your happiness in someone else's hands.

They'll drop it.

They'll drop it every time."

Christopher Barzak

WHAT IS LEADING WITH STONE HEART?

Leadership with Stone Heart is about self-sustainability.

Great leaders understand that they don't need help from others in order to be energised; they can energise themselves. Stone Heart in leadership demonstrates self-sustenance in action. People turn to leaders who are calm and controlled. People turn to leaders whom they see as energy sources. When we learn to energise from within ourselves, we become leaders.

Leadership with Stone Heart is about applying leadership to yourself. It's the self-reflection part of leadership. It's the turning in.

In Daniel Goleman's *Primal Leadership*, he considers emotional intelligence – an essential leadership skill – in four quadrants: self-awareness, self-management, social awareness, and relationship management[8]. The first two domains are placed under the wider bracket of personal competence. Self-awareness is the ability to make an accurate self-assessment, while self-management concerns emotional self-control, transparency, adaptability, and optimism. These components essentially correspond to those of Stone Heart. They are the components of learning how to lead oneself.

When you look to others to energise you, it's your ego asking for external validation. If you don't realise that, you haven't yet mastered your mind. Not to worry, it's a work in progress! Spend some more time processing the material in the previous chapters, particularly around ego.

External validation energises us because it makes us feel like we are worthwhile, like what we've been doing is worthwhile. And yet, what is the implication of that? If you don't receive that validation, then your work wasn't worthwhile? You're asking another person to find meaning in your experience. Yet your experience has meaning regardless of who is there to witness it.

The moment you seek external validation, you express your incompleteness and lack of self-confidence. You're admitting the desire to act according to a perspective that isn't your own, waiting for opinions and ego to be projected onto you rather than forging your own path.

Instead, turn inward. Stone Heart asks you to find meaning in your current circumstance without input from others. The answers already exist within. It's time to trust your self.

Why is Leading with Stone Heart so Important?

The ability to sustain your own energy and heal independently is essential for self-mastery. To self-sustain, you must be able to turn in. When you turn in, you discover the intelligence that was there all along. You can solve problems simply by closing your eyes, returning to yourself, and connecting with your inner well of energy and wisdom. All the information you need is right there – you just need to turn in and find it.

Once you can access all the energy and information you need from within, you become independent of any outside factors. This builds your ability to lead calmly regardless of the external world, and establishes you as a leader whom others can turn to.

Stone Heart is the inner strength that enables you to lead. It is your inner source of energy and love. As we will soon learn, Light Heart involves reflecting this inner energy and love outwards to also give energy to those we are leading – but first we need to find the source within ourselves.

Throughout life, your energy is going to wax and wane. Leading with Stone Heart requires you to fill your own cup.

Temperament tests like introversion/extroversion assessments and the Myers-Briggs Type Indicator can be fun. People love to label themselves. But the results of these tests are not absolute truths; they are only assessments of the ego. Whether you're a quiet lone wolf or a talkative social butterfly, you need to be able to detach and re-energise. And you need to be able to do this regardless of your surroundings. The idea that your environment is responsible for energising or de-energising you is just another framework controlling you. That's not who you are.

Consider a time when your leadership environment became chaotic. How did you respond? How did that response make your team feel, and what was the ultimate outcome?

If you're like many leaders, you may have let the stress get to you. Perhaps your knee-jerk responses led to miscommunications or upset team members. Ultimately, the disruptive energy you created probably caused dissonance in your team, making it hard for any of you to see a way out. This is an example of poor leadership. Internalising surrounding chaos only perpetuates the problem you are trying to solve, as the inner chaos reflects back as further outer chaos in what soon becomes an endless vicious cycle.

If you were able to instead detach from the chaos and turn inward, you could have chosen your response. Rather than compounding the stress, you could have buoyed your team with a response that was calm, hopeful, clear, and energised. Leading with Stone Heart enables you to energise and problem solve from within, spreading calm rather than chaos.

LEAD WITH STONE HEART BY ENERGISING FROM WITHIN

In my early thirties, I hired a business coach. We worked together for five years, focusing on my management and leadership skills. I needed this coach. Whenever I faced a challenge, I would call him to vent, he'd calm me down, and we'd talk it through. As my Stone Heart grew, the phone calls became less frequent. I began to solve my own problems. I began to energise from within. Great leaders are self-sufficient. They make decisions with their executives and partners, but they energise themselves.

Growing up, I observed my father's ability to self-entertain. Sometimes he would sit with a book all day. I remember him telling teenage me, "Put me in a hole and I can be happy!" in village-style Cypriot. I'm grateful to him for this lesson in self-sustainability.

Many high-performing athletes, mega-stars, and well-known CEOs extol the virtues of meditation practices, and with good reason. Meditation comes in many forms: mindfulness, practising gratitude, closed eyes, prayer, Transcendental Meditation, movement, listening to music, breath work… the list goes on. But in all its forms, meditation is essentially a tool for energising from within. It offers a new level of independence because it teaches the soul to neutralise emotions and solve problems internally.

Leadership with Stone Heart is about turning in. One must know where their well of energy and love sits before they can draw from it. If it sits on the outer plane, it's near impossible to practise Stone Heart, Light Heart. The energy and love you give on the outer plane must come from within you. Meditation and stillness will enable this.

Imagine what would happen to our world if we each learned to energise from within. As a collective, we would be more self-sustaining. We would problem-solve our own personal issues, we would be more aware of the energetic impact we have on others, and we would spend more time becoming complete within ourselves. The outcome of all of this would be less drama, and more joy.

Sometimes people ask me, "Gosh, Stella, where do you get your energy from? How do you do so much?"… the answer is simple! I practise Stone Heart. I am my own energy source. I don't wait for others to give me love, guidance, acceptance, or validation; I give them to myself. And I have enough left over to also give enormous amounts of energy, love, and connection to the people I care about. In return, though I don't rely on it, I also accept love and energy – and the well continues to fill.

To experience love from someone, you must first love yourself. Why? Because your perception of love from others is based upon your perception of self.

When you can fill your own well, it doesn't mean your well can't still be topped up by the love of others. You can still exchange energy with others, and you should – this is one of the great joys of life. The difference is, you don't *need* to suck it from others. You *can* function without it. You can independently energise yourself.

Turning inward is the foundation for everything I teach. When the student can call upon themselves for every answer, they no longer need me – they have become their own teacher.

Taming the Animals in the Office

Stop feeding the bird

I've held many one-on-one meetings that have been interrupted by animals. Often, a staff member will sit opposite me with a bird perched quite blatantly on their shoulder. You might be familiar with this kind of bird – the kind that gossips in your ear, reminds you that action leads to failure, and assures you of your inadequacy. The elaborate emotional dance these birds perform can send the victim into a limbic frenzy. I've witnessed the bird induce anxiety attacks, crying fits, rage, violence, abuse, even self-harm.

When you put the bird in charge, you lose control, perspective, and any ability to think rationally.

The bird is a representation of your monkey mind's unconscious patterns and beliefs. If your unconscious patterns and beliefs are unserving, your bird will be like a vulture, eating away at your life. The bird will tell you all sorts of stories and untruths about your world and share destructive judgments and opinions about you and those around you. It's easy to buy into these stories, to be intoxicated by the gossip, all the while unaware of the slippery slope you're on.

The bird is the voice of your ego. It's not you. Sometimes it says good stuff, sometimes it says bad stuff. Either way, it's just your ego talking, spouting the flavour of the moment. You never need to listen to this.

Everyone has a bird. Until, that is, they stop feeding it, whereupon it begins to wither away. Stone Heart asks you to become aware of when you are listening to and acting in alignment with the bird, and to deliberately detach from it. To detach is to remove the bird's food supply. In this way, masters of Stone Heart, Light Heart are ultimately able to kill the bird altogether.

The difference between a highly resonant leader and an average leader is the power they devolve to their bird. I used to be a less-than-average leader. My bird ran the show. Every decision I made was driven by what the bird had to say. Every move I made, the bird would question it. It took me many years to learn that I must shoot the bird on sight. In leadership, attachment to your monkey mind makes you nothing but a perch for a more primitive leader.

I'll ask again: who's in charge – you or the zoo?

Highly resonant leaders are able to silence the bird and enjoy balanced emotions as a result. They don't peak and trough all day; they stay calm and consistent. We are naturally attracted to these leaders because their energy is high. When we hang out with them, we feel good.

Developing awareness of and detachment from your bird is an important part of leading with Stone Heart. Replace that inner voice with a conscious affirmation and work hard at keeping your inner world in order. When you do, that order will be reflected in your outer world.

Scorpions will be scorpions

In leadership, we are often charged with people development and bringing out the best in others. Our job is to build a community of like-minded people in the interest of a common goal and vision. But what happens when an individual behaves repeatedly in a way that is destructive to your community and its goals, despite your best efforts? Where do we draw the line in our acceptance, so as not to accept negative behaviour?

If a person has repeatedly exhibited 'bad' behaviour despite your best efforts to teach them your version of better, you must accept that as their truth. It's possible to accept their behaviour while still asking them to leave. Leadership with Stone Heart allows us to detach so we can love and not judge the individual while protecting our values.

The only thing you can control is yourself. You can't change other people's behaviours; only they can. Anyway, who are you to project your judgment of wrong and right onto a person? That's *your* judgment. They have already shown you their truth, and it's not your place to try to play God in their life. However, if their behaviours don't line up with your leadership values, they are showing you that they simply don't fit into your tribe right now. And that means it's okay to ask them to leave.

Have you ever heard the tale about the scorpion and the frog? It's a fable about a frog who, after careful consideration, chooses to help a scorpion across a river. The scorpion had promised not to sting the frog, since it would mean the end for them both. But halfway across the river, the scorpion does sting the frog, exclaiming, "I couldn't help it, it's in my nature!" and they both sink to the bottom of the river. The moral of the story? Scorpions will be scorpions.

The untamed monkey mind is a scorpion. While we must treat others with kindness and acceptance, we must also beware of those who are still at the mercy of their zoos. Equally, we must beware of those who are in control of their minds but live according to truths that don't align with our own. Everyone is at a different stage of a different journey. Everyone has a different values tree, and that is reflected in their behaviour. When a person demonstrates a certain behaviour time after time, they are showing us their truth, and we must accept it. But acceptance is not the same as tolerance.

As a leader, you need to decide which behaviours you will and will not tolerate in your tribe. Once you have drawn those lines, apply the scorpion rule. Scorpions will be scorpions. Be detached in your application of this rule or you will be stung again and again, with no one to blame but yourself.

The Power of Perspective

Things aren't always as they seem. If you saw an ape belting out a drum solo, would you believe your eyes? It would be hard, because we understand that apes can't play the drums. But if you could only *hear* the ape playing the drums (and not see it), you wouldn't judge your perception – you would simply enjoy the music.

Your mind is constantly deceiving you. It constructs your experience moment to moment based on what your five senses are picking up, and produces a projection of reality filtered through your preconceived ideas and judgments. When we live from our minds, we often lose the magic of the moment.

When you are fantasising about sex, imagining whatever floats your boat, you can quickly reach orgasm. Are the scenarios you imagine real? They are real in your head, and you are having a real experience.

Reality exists in the mind of the viewer.

Let's take another look at the drumming scenario, this time from the ape's perspective. In the ape's fixed reality, it's normal for an ape to play the drums. That's the ape's perception. But it's still just a perception.

Everyone has their own fixed perceptions. We all experience the 'same' moment through various filters, and we each perceive a different reality. There is no one reality. Reality is created in the mind of the viewer, which means we are creating our experiences moment to moment.

Reality is an infinite field of potential.

Understanding this will enable you to become more creative in your experience of life. You can choose your own reality, creating the perception you desire in your mind then projecting that perception onto your experience of the world.

You are in charge of your reality. You are the sole curator of your life.

But you are not the centre of the universe.

Control what you can, accept what you can't

It's hard to accept that we are not the centre of the universe. We might be the centre of our own universe, but we are not the centre of *the* universe. We live in a world where there is very little we can control. We can't control the weather, the seasons, the traffic, our angry boss, a barking dog, or the spider in the car. The world around us is chaotic, and increasingly so.

I can't help but hear my mother's voice: "Back in my day, we didn't have telephones; we had patience." When I am an elder, what will I be saying to my kids? It's hard to imagine life in 40 years' time. All I know is, whatever it throws at us, I won't have the chance to control it. The only thing I can control in this world is me. I am the CEO of my world, and I work very hard to keep that position. Stone Heart, Light Heart will enable you to be the CEO of yours.

I often meet people who are not the CEOs of their own lives – people who have handed the position over to their egos, best friends, parents or spouses. Like puppets, their thoughts and emotions are at the mercy of others. Turn inward often to check who is in charge of you. If you are feeling down, angry, frustrated or scared, turn in and check who you've allowed to shape those emotions. Who gave you the belief system you're working from? Who caused your insecurity? Who prompted you to take action that didn't align with your truth? By turning in, you can establish whether you're actually in charge, or whether you've let someone else take the reins.

In any given moment, turning in can bring you straight back into power. Even if you find your current position to be a result of someone else's model of the world, that's okay. By recognising that, you reclaim control.

By acknowledging that you are not the centre of the universe, you take the pressure off yourself. You can't change the laws of cause and effect, gravity, seasons, sound, or light. So remove the weight of the world from your shoulders. Recognise that the only thing that you can control is yourself. Take ownership of how you turn up to life and how you experience every moment, for each moment is as valuable as your first and your last.

STONE HEART, LIGHT HEART

I am not the centre of the universe.

To help build perspective in times of pressure or challenge, try using the five-year question and the 24-hour question. I find these two questions so helpful, especially if the moment has something to do with my kids or family – for example, if I need to cancel a work meeting to be at the school. At first I might feel immense diary stress and pressure. But then I apply the two questions.

When you feel challenged, ask yourself:

Will this moment matter in five years?

Will the meeting I'll have to miss matter in five years? Hell no! But if I don't go to the school and see my baby get an award? Hell yeah. So the decision is actually pretty simple – and I can let the pressure over my diary start to lift. The chaos is still there. I haven't changed the chaos. But I have changed how I *respond* to the chaos. I've considered what matters most to me, and taken charge to make the right decision and reduce my stress. If I remained stressed, who would be in charge of my world? My diary.

In times of acute stress, your limbic brain is triggering the release of heaps of cortisol, plunging your body into the fight/flight/freeze response. And it could take you a few hours to get out of that. So if you're struggling to come to a decision, ask yourself the second key question:

Can this decision wait 24 hours?

If it can, it should. Give those hormones a chance to flush out of your system. Don't make decisions when the monkey is in charge or they will be animal decisions, not carefully considered decisions. You can see these animal responses in full swing when you get copied into corporate email ping pong. Aggro emails get hurled back and forth, with no highly evolved thought or communication to be seen.

It's a classic leadership fail when you let the monkey take control. Most events and decisions can afford 24 hours to allow for sound calm decision making. Take the time.

Stone Heart in Summary

Stone Heart can be summarised by two actions: love and detachment. Love for self and others. Detachment from thoughts and judgments.

Reprogram your mind using affirmations to build yourself an armour of self-love. Incoming bullets may impact your energetic field momentarily, but your energy will quickly bounce back unharmed.

Accept the law of failure so that you can detach from ego. You are not the centre of the universe. You are, however, the centre of your universe. With this understanding, you must vow to take charge of the one thing that you can control: yourself.

When a person judges you, look for where they are operating from – their true self or their ego? You'll quickly learn that judgment necessarily stems from ego. Once you understand this, you can carry a bright light of love and detachment towards others.

Take a conscious step towards detachment to ensure that low vibrational energies do not impact your energetic world. When you are not able to detach, you absorb the energies of those around you and lose touch with the *I* within. My wish for you is that no matter what energy crosses your path, you have the inner wisdom to hold your own. You are the master of your world. No one else.

Stone Heart gives you strength and courage, quashing fear. Fear is the monkey mind trying to protect us. But we don't want protection, we want propulsion! Fortunately, we can deconstruct fear with affirmations and rewiring.

I continually seek fearful journeys, expecting failure and rejoicing in the opportunity it brings. My acceptance of the fail-recover-grow cycle allows me to embrace failure as my friend. I succeed only through repeated trial and error.

Stone Heart is a clearing of the weeds in the mind, getting the mind in order so that Light Heart can awaken. While Stone Heart often concerns itself with everyday life events, Light Heart connects more deeply with who you are and why you are here.

Light Heart is a new dimension altogether. It is the god consciousness within you, and it is extremely powerful. When we unmask ourselves using Stone Heart, we can freely play with the energies of Light Heart. With time and practice, Light Heart will awaken more and more.

Light Heart is where love sits. Acceptance of life and death. Joy in the silence. Passion and energy for your calling. It is subtle and mystical, and it has a sense of wonderment and magic about it. When it awakens in you, you gain a sense of connection to the universe that lets you know you are okay.

Light Heart is the calm, the love, the all-knowingness within. Combining Stone Heart and Light Heart allows you to connect with the master within. The power that you are born with. The power to create with love and detachment, and to vibrate with peace and joy in every moment.

Stone Heart, Light Heart in Action

Reflect on your leadership at work and answer the following questions:

Where do I get my energy from?

. . . .
. . . .

When I am flat, what do I do to recharge?

. . . .
. . . .

Do I have a way to energise that is independent of others?

. . . .
. . . .

When faced with a challenge, what does the voice in my head say?

. . . .
. . . .

Do I have a bird?

. . . .
. . . .

What does the bird say?

. . . .
. . . .

Am I inhibited by the bird in any way?

. . . .
. . . .

Do I have any scorpions in my team?

. . . .
. . . .

Am I tolerant of their behaviour?

. . . .
. . . .

Are they stinging me and others?

. . . .
. . . .

Can I do anything about it?

. . . .
. . . .

Do I have a rule in place that helps me to safeguard my decisions from my monkey brain?

. . . .
. . . .

Your answers here will give you a heat map on how you apply Stone Heart in leadership and alert you to any areas that you can tweak.

SECTION TWO:
LIGHT HEART

I am in charge of my reality, and so I become the curator of my life.

Chapter 6

Awakening Light Heart

"We shape clay into a pot, but it is the emptiness inside that holds whatever we want."

Lao Tzu

Getting mystical

So much of what we have spoken about so far has been about mastering your three minds and reprogramming your unconscious thoughts and habits into templates of thinking that accelerate you in life. But this book isn't only about mastery of the mind; this book is also about mastery of the self. I want to now open your mind to the world and reality that exists beyond the mind. There is something mystical, even supernatural about embracing greater awareness of yourself and who you are in this world and beyond. Light Heart is about awakening to the mystical within you.

What Is Light Heart?

Light Heart is consciousness itself. It's the awareness we have after removing the lens of ego. Unlike Stone Heart, Light Heart is not a framework. It is the presence of who you are; the presence that exists between your thoughts.

We can gain an understanding of what this space between our thoughts is by considering the beautiful Japanese concept of *Ma*. This refers to the empty space between things, and how this space is often as important as the thing itself. In this space we find potential, and creative possibility. The very fact that there *is* a space is what allows us to engage with our imagination and the unknown, as we find creative ways to use and fill that space.

In this clear space lies connection with the internal. Light Heart doesn't have a structure; it is infinite. It is difficult to explain that to a person who lives externally. We must let go of the external if we are to find the beautiful nothingness of the internal.

Meditation is a practice of Light Heart. When we meditate and quiet our mind, turning off the ego completely, we create the space to connect with who we truly are.

Why is Light Heart so important?

There is one thing that can colour your entire life and stop you from being free and joyful, and that is your attachment to ego.

When we learn to disconnect from ego, something remarkable happens: we become more aware. Our senses sharpen. We have more wisdom. We make quicker decisions. We feel inspired. When we stop thinking, we become aware of the consciousness that exists around us. Try it right now: bring your attention to your thoughts. Now bring your attention to the space between each of those thoughts. That space is awareness.

In any moment, even with chaos around you, you can find completeness and peace. When you awaken Light Heart, you access this capacity. In *Man's Search for Meaning*, Viktor Frankl, who endured life in a concentration camp during the Holocaust, wrote, "Everything can be taken from a man but one thing: the last of the human freedoms – to choose one's attitude in any given set of circumstances, to choose one's own way."[9] This is the ultimate expression of self-mastery. Essentially, this is what we're all seeking – to become complete within ourselves. We want to have inner peace and to experience love. No human truly seeks to experience anything more than that, it is only our ego that seeks to convince us we do.

Light Heart is important because it allows us to experience this inner peace no matter what is going on around us. If you can learn Light Heart, you don't need to become "enlightened". You don't need to become a monk or have a special lightbulb moment. The word *enlightenment* conveys a sudden realisation of the meaning of life. But if you understand life for one moment, does that mean you're all set?

Your life will change continuously, and your experiences and perceptions will change with it. Light Heart is a continual process of being connected to oneself. It allows you to reach enlightenment again and again as you learn and grow, rather than reaching it once as though it were a final destination.

This is the foundation of self-mastery.

AWAKEN LIGHT HEART BY EMBRACING THE PRESENT MOMENT

If you want to experience complete self-mastery, you must master the concept of the present moment – what Dr Joe Dispenza refers to as the "eternal now".[10] There is a lot of talk about being present right now, there are many books being written on it, and many meditation techniques that can help you become present. But first I want to look a little deeper into what it actually *means* to be present.

While most people understand the idea of being present through conscious thought, I want to offer you a completely different understanding of the concept. This will require you to get beyond the physical world of your body, your aches and pains, your ego, your values and beliefs, your identity, and even time itself. After all, if you can't get beyond who you think you are and who you have been conditioned to be, how can you master yourself and create a new reality for yourself? You can't. To become present, you must elevate above the identity you have constructed for yourself.

In this chapter, I am going to introduce to you the concept of *I*, which is pure consciousness itself. You can't access this space through ego, thought, memories of the past, or fantasies of the future. You can access it only through the present moment. To me, this is what it truly means to be present – to escape from your conscious mind entirely, and simply *be*.

When you are immersed in your day-to-day life, your unconscious habits and patterns are running you. Your brain circuity has been moulded through all your past experiences to help you navigate life, often on autopilot. But while this can be helpful in some ways, it essentially means the way you are operating in the present is based wholly on the past. As your unconscious conditioning dictates your expected future, running the same old, same old, over and over, your past can often become your future – unless you learn to master your mind and self.

I wouldn't want my past to dictate my future, would you? I want new experiences and new ways of being. *Better* ways of being.

If you continue to allow your future to be predicated on your past conditioning, you will be perpetually disappointed. If you are moving through life on autopilot, with your predictable future simply unfolding day by day, how can you make room for new or the unknown aspects of you? You can't.

The only way to let go of past habits and prevent them from translating into future habits is to connect with the unknown aspects of yourself – your pure creative potential, consciousness itself – your inner *I*.

Know Thyself

No one can tell you who you are. Not even your own thoughts can tell you who you are, as they are no more than mental constructs. Your drama, your problems, your fears, your fantasies… none of these are who you are. Those ideas come and go. There is a you that is deeper than your ideas.

Stone Heart is knowing *about* yourself; Light Heart is actually *knowing yourself*. The latter has nothing to do with context or facts about your life.

To know who you are, you must begin by knowing who you are not. This means letting go of the parts of you that can be attributed to your external world. These may have been parts of your identity – your sense of self – for many years. But the time has come to let them go.

If you only see the tangible in life, your life will be very competitive and lack meaning and enjoyment. Focusing on objects and things takes us out of the present moment, and away from the spiritual dimension. As hard as it might sound, to be fully present you must let go of everything tangible that currently defines you, and of any ideas or thoughts about the past or the future. This will draw all your awareness to what's going on around you right now, allowing you to observe the present moment in its infinite beauty, without judgment or attachment.

Your ego blocks you from changing your identity, whereas Light Heart enables detachment from it and therefore flexibility around it. Ideally, we can practise this awareness of self no matter where we are. Sometimes, however, it takes an external experience to prompt us to see that we have been trapped by the external world.

A friend of mine experienced a form of awakening after a cultural exchange of some months in Japan. Growing up, she had expressed her identity exclusively through jeans and hoodies. Fear of her friends' potential reactions stopped her from changing her style, even when she might have wanted to dress up. When she moved to Tokyo, the physical separation from those friends provided an enforced detachment of sorts from their opinions. She began to experiment with different clothing styles and more feminine looks. The detachment from judgment – from ego – allowed her the freedom to reinvent herself, and to maintain this new identity even when she returned home. The beauty of Light Heart is that it gives you this kind of freedom in every moment.

Why is being flexible with your identity important? Well, first, if you think about it logically, you clearly don't want to be the same person throughout your life (you might have been a cute five-year-old, but do you still want that identity when you're fifteen, or fifty?). Second, attachment to a particular identity limits us from truly knowing ourselves. A set of labels can never encompass the true variety of the human experience. When we let ourselves believe it does, it becomes an excuse to hide behind.

Let's take a look at a more acute example. When you lose a loved one, it might feel like some part of you has also died, leaving a huge void in your life. But you are not your loved one. Following their death, you might create a huge and persistent pain-body called grief. The grief tells you that you cannot be happy. But you are not your grief, either. You can let go of this pain-body through acceptance. Knowing thyself starts with letting go of what you are not: you are not your loved one, you are not the loss of them, and you are not your grief. True acceptance is letting go of all three of these things.

By all means, grieve! But don't let it consume you. Grief can often be a story we tell about how we should feel after losing someone. Detach from this story and seek your own truth. Do not allow yourself to be labelled by your external world. Detachment will give you some peace even when you are sitting in the emptiness. When you find acceptance, the space and emptiness become peace, and from that peace comes a yet deeper sense of acceptance and awareness. If the only thing you can control is yourself, then identifying with the experiences of your past denies you the right to recreate a new future. In the example of grief, it means you never stop grieving.

Knowing yourself is being rooted in your being, rather than lost in your mind. Knowing yourself deeply has nothing to do with the ideas floating around in your mind, even if they're spiritual ideas about who you are. They are merely constructs. True knowing sits deep inside you and goes beyond any rationalised concept of who you are. This is the essence of Stone Heart, Light Heart. Stone Heart enables you to detach from both your ego and your zoo; Light Heart enables you to become rooted in your being, unattached to any external constructs, fully aware and present. Light Heart uses acceptance, joy, and passion to bring you into the present moment. This moment is all there is.

I have a simple experience to share around this. During a fight with my husband, I got into my monkey mind. I was angry and frustrated, and I'd disconnected from myself. To regain Light Heart, I gave my awareness to the state I was in. Right there in that moment, I returned home to myself through meditation. I felt the love in my heart. I looked through my husband's lens to connect with his highest self. And I started seeing him not as a source of frustration but as a magnificent being, just as I am. I felt an unconditional love for myself, which I was then able to extend to him. I asked myself what it was that I needed to do to bring peace to the moment. The answer from within was to simply to walk up to him, hold him by the shoulders, and say, "I want to let you know that I've meditated. I've come back home. I want to apologise for the disconnection, and I want to love and cuddle you. Then, I'd like to have a discussion about what happened."

It's really important to note here that by going away and taking back control of my energy, I didn't magically resolve the entire argument. What I did was resolve my ego and regain control of my mind. My husband and I still needed to discuss and solve the problem, but now we could do it from a place of alignment. This meant we could navigate the problem more easily, with kindness and respect.

It sounds too easy, doesn't it? Actually, most people find this sort of resolution extremely difficult. Consider how you'd feel about saying, "I've meditated on this. I'm letting go of the ego that was attached to it. I love you. Let's talk about that moment." If it'd make you feel uncomfortable, if you'd feel a tension or a mental block, then your ego is still in the way. That's why all the work earlier in the book is so important. Don't panic about your own resistance. Just go back and re-read the parts you need to on detachment and finding Stone Heart. Then, try again.

As you practise Stone Heart, Light Heart, you will gain confidence in knowing who you are and who you are not. You will stop seeking validation from the external world. You will instead turn in to validate yourself. You will turn in to make decisions.

I have an acquaintance who consistently seeks validation from others. He won't make a decision on anything until he has socialised his ideas, which essentially means the decisions he ultimately implements are no longer his. When I ask him what he thinks, he'll say, "I don't know, what do you think?". This habit is disempowering. To have power, one must realise that the power sits within. Power cannot be sourced externally; if you have to look for it, you don't have it.

Spend time and energy daily on getting to know yourself and mastering the *I* within. Take time to experience the difference between who you think you are and who you really are. Who you think you are is a function of ego, subject to change depending on your current mental filters. Who you really are sits in the silence between your thoughts; it is consciousness itself.

So when you master Stone Heart, Light Heart and conquer ego, is there still a gap between who you think you are and who you really are?

The gap between who you are and who you think you are can never truly be closed, because who you are is not something that can necessarily be put into thoughts or words. Who you are must be *experienced*. Rather, as you master your mind and yourself, you will let go of the very construct of "who you think you are" because you understand that the ego is just a construct, subject to change. It's not who you are. It's merely a template you have constructed over time.

Who you are sits behind that. When you strip away the layers of ego all the way back to nothing, you will experience a space where nothing exists but your own awareness. This is consciousness. When you access this space of consciousness, you will find who you are. This is a powerful experience, and you are likely to experience immense love, self-love and peace. In this space, you can draw on your limitless personal energy and creative potential to reimagine your life and your goals, and solve any and all problems.

Pure energy and creative potential. Boundless love. Sounds good, doesn't it? Getting to know yourself really is your most important job here on Earth. If we could all master the *I* within, the world would be a more peaceful place.

I started my personal journey of self-mastery at the age of 12, when I read *Bring Out the Magic of Your Mind*[11]. Since then, I have attended dozen of seminars and workshops and read hundreds of books on self-empowerment. I have gathered information from the outside world and implemented it in my inside world. I now have enough tools under my belt that I don't need to look out anymore. I just turn in. Channelling knowledge through meditation is my most evolved way of seeking answers. This is power. The well within me is full because I keep it that way. And I'm teaching my daughters to do the same. This is the most important thing I am teaching them: to practise Stone Heart, Light Heart in everything they do.

Spot Your Ego and Stop It in Its Tracks

If knowing yourself is about detaching from the ego, then your first task is to build greater awareness of your ego. From here, the rest will cascade, as you simply cannot remain in your ego once you have become aware of it.

The moment you spot your ego is the moment you become aware. And when you are aware, you can be truly present.

Spot your ego and stop it in its tracks by looking out for the following behaviours in yourself:

- ❖ **Reacting**. Reactions are essentially split-second judgments. These judgments often reflect our insecurities. For example, when you witness another person's greed, the intensity of your reaction to it is an indication of how greedy you feel *you* are. When you react to something, you create a space for this same thing to exist within yourself.

- ❖ **Complaining**. Complaining is a form of attachment. It strengthens the ego. If you continuously criticise and judge your situation, wishing you could be in a different one, ego is commandeering your thoughts.

- ❖ **Name calling**. We label not just individuals, but whole cultures and societies. When we label people, we desensitise ourselves to their humanity. In fact, it is our own ego talking, desiring to put ourselves above them and build confidence through (false) superiority.

- ❖ **Giving judgmental feedback**. If your comments are laced with ego, the receiver will detect the negative motive, triggering an egoic response from them, too. End this cycle before it begins by considering where your feedback is coming from before you deliver it. Aim to give non-judgmental feedback by stating objective facts in a constructive manner.

- ❖ **Worrying**. Worry is a function of the ego. No matter how much you worry, it will never, in itself, bring about change. Get out of that pattern of unconscious worrying by connecting with yourself a few times a day. Meditating and bringing awareness to the present moment will help you regularly find that connection and aliveness though presence.

- ❖ **Overthinking.** When your thoughts are constantly moving, it's your ego talking. On a spiritual level, you are unconscious. Your job is to become conscious.

When you identify with your internal emotional state, you are allowing your ego to dominate. Aggression, anger, sadness, and all other emotions arise in the limbic brain. So to strengthen Light Heart, we need to consistently recognise when we are emotional. Similarly, when you identify with your opinions and viewpoints, you identify with your ego. This is not who you are.

The behaviours that you act out directly relate to your thoughts, which is why you must take time to reflect on your thoughts often. Detach from them so that you no longer identify with the drama and the emotion. This creates more space for you to enjoy life.

ACCEPT THE PRESENT

Make accepting and embracing the present moment your primary objective, always. This is the only moment you have, and therefore it is your life. To reject the present moment is to reject life itself. If you encounter something unpleasant, your challenge is to accept the moment as if you have chosen it. Because it's the only one you have.

How can you enjoy a crappy day? Through acceptance and mastery of the judgments you have projected onto it. After all, is it really crappy? Or is that just a judgment from the mind? Accelerate Light Heart by stepping outside such stories.

Imagine you are standing in a long, slow line at the supermarket. You have somewhere important to be in just a few minutes, so you begin to get frustrated. This frustration builds in your mind and shifts your energy negatively. As soon as this happens, you lose your edge.

Now imagine that instead, you consciously choose to accept the present moment as the only moment you have in life. You know you can't change it, but you can choose how you interact with it. So you accept it, and through this acceptance comes an inner peace and a disconnection from the ego's story. This inner peace literally changes your reality, because after all, reality is no more than a perception. When you bring acceptance to the present moment, you can find enjoyment in simply being.

Where this becomes tricky is when you are faced with immensely painful challenges – when your child is born with a disability, for example, or you are diagnosed with a terminal illness. How do we accept these challenges in life?

I am a firm believer that those born with disabilities also have a gift, which they also share with their families. I believe every human being has a mission and purpose here on Earth – sick and disabled people as much as any other. I do not judge this circumstance, but embrace and accept it as the only circumstance I can embrace and accept. Some of the happiest families I know have a disabled family member. They are real and connected.

I am not an expert in death; nor is anyone. I saw many people pass from illness during my days as a medical student, and I also saw many people heal themselves from so-called "terminal" illness. When I was in my intern year, my mum was diagnosed with stage-four thyroid cancer. She underwent surgery and radiation therapy, which saw her placed in solitary confinement for a week. My mum is alive and well. Part of her healing was spiritual; it started with acceptance. Acceptance of the cancer, and recognition of its potential blessing.

It was soon after Mum's diagnosis that I quit my job and started Mind Connection. Mum was my first patient. We worked together to find her inner *I* by accepting the present moment. Healing cannot happen in past thoughts or future fantasies. Healing happens in the present moment, through connection to spirit.

The body is a magnificent vehicle, capable of remarkable healing. Your job is to connect with it in the present moment and to be its guide. It will then share with you the discords, blocks, anxieties, and challenges that you are holding on to at the level of your unconscious. Your job is to uncover the truth beyond these barricades by taking the time to actually look. Bring forth your Stone Heart, Light Heart. During this process, your body will respond with energetic healing. Physical healing begins with the mind.

The magic of healing begins when we accept that the illness is ours to heal.

The magic of happiness begins when we accept our current circumstance, whatever it may be, and find peace knowing it is all we have.

The magic of forgiveness begins when we accept that the event we faced could only have happened in that way.

You are responsible for the state of your own consciousness. If you cannot accept your present, you need to stop what you are doing and take immediate action. If you do not, you are choosing to neglect responsibility for your own life.

Escape the Trap of Happiness

Part of accepting the present moment is embracing both happiness and sadness, and recognising that they are transient.

If you cling to a happy situation, will you then be unhappy by comparison when it passes (as it inevitably will)? When we cling to happiness, we become attached to it, and that can be just as damaging as becoming attached to ideas or objects. When we are attached to happiness, a lack of happiness automatically engenders sadness. Worse, even in the presence of happiness, we can be hampered by a fear of losing that happiness.

If you are going through some challenges, know that this too shall pass. Allow change to happen and become comfortable with it, for it is the only constant.

Get Outside the Stories

Sometimes we feel totally consumed by the busyness of life. Busyness can create a backlog of challenges and drama. For example, you might get a flat tyre on the way to work. Flustered, you then spill your coffee on your shirt. When you finally get to work, you open your emails only to find a complaint regarding some of your recent work. As you sit there miserably in your coffee-stained shirt, the panic and negative thinking start to set in. It's barely gone 9-am and already your day has been ruined by the drama. This negative energy sends you into a downward spiral, attracting more negative events and propelling people away from you as you manifest more and more of your funk.

This happens all the time. Work environments are rife with this spiral pattern. The impact of little dramas like spilled coffee can be disproportionately huge. So it's important for us to understand how we can get outside of the stories in our heads.

Imagine you have a broken mirror in front of you and your job is to piece it back together. As you do, you see your own reflection repeated over and over. Each shard is a different shape, reflecting a different perspective of who you are. The stories and judgments in your head are like the shards of the mirror. Each reflects only its own perception. When you're busy, you may find you have lots of different voices in your head telling you what to do or what's going to happen next. Many people start to spiral as they find themselves attaching to all sorts of conflicting thoughts.

When this happens, it can feel like the *I* inside you is not even there. No one's home. The essence of who you are fragments as you simultaneously identify with multiple different stories swimming around your head.

Meditation will collapse all your fragments into one. The simple act of becoming aware of the fragments already helps you start to detach from your stories. As you consciously further that detachment and move into a state of meditation, you will find a deep stillness. That stillness gives birth to what I call the "I am" presence.

The "I am" presence is consciousness itself – there is nothing beyond it. In the "I am" presence, we feel a deep connection to our source energy. This fills us with vibrational energy, awakening acceptance of the present moment and appreciation of what we have.

When you become an observer of the thoughts in your mind rather than allowing them to control you, you increase your vibrational frequency (the physical manifestation of your inner energy – you'll learn more about this in the next chapter). This will result in greater enjoyment of life and faster manifestation of the outcomes you seek.

Breathe In

Breathing. The mystery that divides life from death.

Our first breath signifies our arrival into the world. We are alive. We are born. We are here.

Our last breath signifies our departure. We have passed. We have died. We are no longer here.

Breath is the main vehicle that carries our energy throughout life. It's the constant thread from birth to death.

Our breath has mysterious power. It is our very own personal energy generator. When you are tired, all it takes is one minute of conscious breathing to reoxygenate your brain, and before you know it you are re-energised. When you are anxious, your breathing becomes shallow and rapid, limiting oxygen to your brain and exacerbating tension in the body. Here again, applying breathing techniques can slow the heart rate, reoxygenate the body, and relax the nervous system.

Controlling your breathing is the key to controlling your body and the mind, and the vehicle that connects you to your spirit.

My questions to you are:

- ❖ Have you mastered the power of your breath?
- ❖ When your energy is low, do you use your breath to bring it back up?

Your breath is the vehicle by which you can disconnect from your mind and ego and reconnect with your deeper sense of self. Your breath is the vehicle by which you can become a commanding force in your life. Your breath is the mysterious secret ingredient to awakening Light Heart, strengthening Light Heart, and accelerating Light Heart.

When you align with your breath, you align with yourself by disconnecting from your thoughts, your mind, and your ego. Learning how to breathe for different outcomes is fundamental to living well, both physically and spiritually.

I learned how to breathe during my time with my shaman teacher. She was never interested in hearing my stories, or my projections of whatever emotional rollercoaster I was on. Whenever I went to see her she would simply greet me and say, "Let's breathe".

She would then guide me through a series of breathing drills. Ten minutes would pass, then twenty – still we would be actively breathing. Then she would ask me to open my eyes. "Hello, Stella", she would say softly. "Now I can see you. Talk to me from your heart." I learned from these moments that active breathing completely disconnects you from your mind. She refused to ever talk to me about egoic issues; we would only ever talk from a place of *I*.

I carry the techniques I learned from my wonderful teacher through my every day. I use them to detach from my ego just as I would use a knife to butter bread, or a toothbrush to brush my teeth.

Let's take a look at a few breathing techniques you can implement in your own life. Depending on your needs, you may use one, some, or even all of these breathing techniques to help you practise the philosophies of Stone Heart, Light Heart.

Box breath

Box breath is a great technique for increasing oxygen and mindfulness. It brings you back to the present.

Inhale to the count of four, hold to the count of four, exhale to the count of four. Repeat.

Falling breath

Falling breathing is a great way to destress your body and let go of physical tension.

Take a deep breath, inhaling as much air as possible. At the top of your breath, take three more gasps of air. Then let the breath fall: exhale with a big sigh. Repeat.

Breathe and hold

This is a meditation breathing technique that completely disconnects you from your mind and brings you into a space where you can connect with your inner *I*. When I want to meditate and start connecting with my psychic intuition, I use this technique. Some of my greatest awakenings have come by doing this for 20 minutes.

Inhale as deeply as you can and hold for ten seconds. Then let your breath fall and hold the empty breath for ten seconds. Now fulfil that need to reoxygenate by taking a deep breath of air again… and repeat.

Empty and full breath

This technique activates the parasympathetic nervous system, which stimulates your organs to enter into a relaxed state.

Inhale to the count of three, then exhale to the count of six, focusing on emptying your lungs as much as possible. Repeat.

Shamanic breathing

This breathing technique will take you straight to the "gateway" of consciousness, where three-dimensional reality becomes distant and unimportant, and you instead work with energy and consciousness. From this meditative state you can tap into your wisdom and access the information you need to solve your problems. This is where the power lives, where you can truly build a relationship with the inner *I*. It is my absolute favourite place to go. This technique becomes more valuable as your self-mastery improves.

Breathe in and out through your nose in short, sharp bursts as quickly as you can. Essentially you are hyperventilating with conscious intention. Shamanic breathing can only be used for about 30–60 seconds, as it causes a dizzy, giddy feeling.

You don't need to make active breathing a big thing. Active breathing is extremely simple, as natural as walking or jumping. It's just a thing. But the power it provides you with is enormous. So, next time you find yourself caught up in stress or a little too much ego, stop, and breathe. In, and out. This will bring you back home.

AWAKEN THE INNER WISDOM

Awaken the inner wisdom that lies dormant inside you. You already possess it, it's just that it may be repressed by your monkey mind. It's time to let it bubble up to the surface.

Acceptance is at the core of your awakening. Acceptance, first, that there is no single reality. It's ignorant to assume that your own fixed perceptions, judgments, and assessments of reality are the only valid perceptions. Is this book fixated in one reality? No. One person's interpretation of this book will no doubt be different to the next person's.

The truth is that reality is created in the mind of the viewer, which means we are each creating our own experience – our own reality – moment to moment. Reality is an infinite field of potential, created and maintained by your consciousness.

You must awaken to this. When you do, the paradigms in your life will start to collapse in on themselves as you realise that they are not real. They are frameworks, rules, regulations, and stories built to keep you operating in a system.

I am in charge of my reality. I am the sole curator of my life.

The key to taking charge of your reality is self-mastery. It starts with being aware of the perceptions and filters that shape your interpretation of reality. When you are aware of these perceptions and filters, you can detach from them. When you detach from these perceptions and filters, you take charge of your own reality. And when you take charge of your own reality, you become the curator of your life.

STONE HEART, LIGHT HEART IN ACTION

Set a timer for 60 seconds. Press play, and do a 60-second meditation in which you bring your awareness to the space between your thoughts. Notice your thoughts, but remain detached from them. Don't judge them. Accept them.

What did you learn?

....
....
....
....
....

Choose one of the breathing exercises. Put on some meditation music and put in your headphones. Set a timer and do some purposeful breathing for five minutes.

What do you sense?

....
....
....
....
....

Note: Breathing is a form of meditation. If you can persist with a breathing exercise for 20 minutes, you will have accessed a space of conscious awareness. In this space you can ask your higher conscious mind to help you solve a problem, or recreate and imagine a new future.

. . . .

. . . .

. . . .

. . . .

. . . .

I accept that this is my moment. The only moment I have in my life.

Chapter 7

Strengthening Light Heart

"Stress is caused by being 'here' but wanting to be 'there'."

Eckhart Tolle

What Is Strengthening Light Heart?

As we now understand, Light Heart is about being present. What does it mean to say we want to strengthen Light Heart, then? What does strengthening our ability to be present mean?

It's impossible to be present 24/7, and we wouldn't want to be. Autopilot is a skill our brains have developed so as to avoid having to process an overwhelming amount of information. We function efficiently as humans because we don't have to think consciously about every action we take. There are also times when we need to imagine the future, or want to reflect on the past.

So strengthening Light Heart is not about being present all the time; rather, it is about strengthening your ability to come back to the present. It's about maintaining control over your own state of consciousness. It's about building consistency in your detachment from ego and from opinion.

Strengthening Light Heart is about becoming hyper-aware of your attachments and egoic judgments, because when you have awareness and presence, you simply cannot remain in your ego. Awareness is the first stage of detachment, and the more often you detach, the stronger your connection to self becomes.

Why is strengthening light heart important?

I am a mum, a Cypriot, a CEO, and a recruiter. But beyond that, who am I? I am the essence of me that's found beneath my ego, my consciousness. My consciousness, which is unlimited in its potential to create – as is yours. Most people identify so strongly with the egoic voice in their head that they constantly allow it to control them. Learning how to stop it in its tracks is truly transformational.

STRENGTHENING LIGHT HEART

The voice in your head, your ego, is not who you are. Strengthening Light Heart is so important because it strengthens the essence of who you are in between your thoughts and without your ego in the way. With a strong Light Heart, you are able to acknowledge the stories your monkey mind tells, silence them, and return home. When you can find presence and connect to your higher self, you have the opportunity to live a more complete life because you are 100% there for every moment.

As a species, humans once shared a deep sense of connection to the oneness of life. Many relics of ancient cultures are suggestive of this sense of connection. And this connection is still alive and well in some cultures. To this day, the Aboriginal tribes of Arnhem Land live their live in connection with the oneness of nature. But over the last few thousand years, as humans have become deeper thinkers, many of us have evolved away from our heart centres – where there was a deep self-knowing and a connectedness to God, Mother Nature, and the land – and towards our minds, where we self-identify based on ego.

As we've shifted from the heart to the mind, humanity has progressed in many ways. But we have also become more mentally sick, because we have forgotten how to connect to our sense of self, to our heart, and to the oneness of all that is.

You are one with all life. You cannot understand this through thought itself; it is not something that can be put into words. Rather, it is something that is felt through the presence between thoughts. By accepting and simply being in the present moment, you connect not just with your true self but with the entire universe.

Even when you are surrounded by chaos or devastation, Light Heart will bring power back to you. But you can't achieve it without first mastering your mind. So many people are still allowing their monkey minds to control them, which is why I'm so passionate about bringing this book forward. Every person who can step out of their monkey mind and into Light Heart is another person living in oneness with who they are. That is how we're going to elevate the consciousness of our planet. If each of us eight billion people detaches from our ego and masters who we are, our collective intelligence will rise. I can already see this happening! We are, as a global collective consciousness, evolving further and further away from ego. This is what the spiritual movement is all about.

Strengthen Light Heart by Aligning Heart and Mind

Since our ancestors first started carving out wood, chiselling stones, and painting on the walls of caves, many humans have shared the belief that the heart guides us through the hard times. This is often a central point in ancient writings and symbology. The ancient Greeks believed the heart was the centre of the soul; the Egyptians believed that the heart, not the brain, was the centre of life and human wisdom; and the Romans believed that the heart was the body's most energy-giving organ. Throughout the ages, humans have continued to believe that heart, beyond its function of pumping blood through the body, is our connection to God or the innate intelligence of the universe.

Over the last 30 years, organisations such as HeartMath Institute have conducted research that supports this belief.[12] Beyond its central role in sustaining life, the heart also communicates with the brain to influence our emotions and cognitive processes, including our understanding of ourselves and our place in the world. By connecting into the heart's inner knowing, we can tap into the wisdom of our consciousness and the source of our own energy.

Biologically, the heart and brain are connected through billions of neurons and complex ascending and descending neural pathways. When the signals coming from the heart are in disharmony with the signals coming from the brain, you split your energy. Your physical energy drops. You lose your power to manifest.

Connection to your inner energy source cannot happen in the mind, only in the heart. When you connect with your heart energy to master Light Heart, the metaphysical space of congruence opens up to you. Congruence is when your mind and heart are completely in alignment with each other. Congruence of mind and heart results in effortless action and flow; in this state, everything seems to just work out.

Incongruence between mind and heart, on the other hand, makes it hard to stay on the right path in life. You might have heard people say, "My head says one thing, but my heart says something else; such moments of friction lead to adversities – accidents, lateness, bad "luck". These adversities might be minor and surmountable, or they might accumulate to cause a sense of dissonance, potentially even leading to mental illness.

To know ourselves, we must unite mind and heart. In order to do this, we must quieten the mind and its judgments in order to hear and feel the energy of the heart.

BEINGNESS

Beingness is the state in which your consciousness is aligned with your true self. To find your beingness, you must break the habit of living through the egoic mind and start living from the heart, in connection with all that is. Through the heart consciousness, you can perceive a much greater existence.

In old age, activity shifts from doing to being. The older you become, the more conscious you become. You come to recognise the value of being. But you don't have to wait until you are approaching death for your consciousness to awaken. All you need to do is connect with your heart.

Consciousness doesn't ignite in the mind; it ignites in the heart when the mind is still, inspiring love and joy. Your egoic mind projects judgments, whereas your heart consciousness projects nothing – it just knows. It is the true *I* inside you. Beingness means being *you*. Connecting to consciousness itself.

Stop interpreting life through your mind. It's totally limiting. Your mind doesn't get it. Instead, start to see life through your heart. In the state of beingness, you connect with your source energy, your intuition expands, and you develop a deep knowing of who you are and why you are here. In this state, you can co-create anything your heart desires.

STEPPING UP YOUR VIBRATIONAL ENERGY

Achieving coherence of mind and heart is a central part of practising Stone Heart, Light Heart. In doing so, we can actually alter the energy we give off into the world.

HeartMath Institute's work is centred around the premise that when an individual marries clear intention (clarity of thought) with elevated emotion (coherent heart), the coherence of the brain-heart connection produces a change in the heart's electromagnetic field.

This means that emotions experienced through the brain-heart connection create a biological frequency of energy in your body, which I like to refer to as your "vibrational energy". The energy frequency may be very high, very low, or anywhere in between, depending on the emotion you are experiencing.

Figure 9, taken from the book *Becoming Supernatural* by Dr Joe Dispenza, depicts the vibrational frequencies of some common emotional states[13]. It's a useful way for us to visualise the vibrational energy we give off as we experience different emotions.

Figure 9.

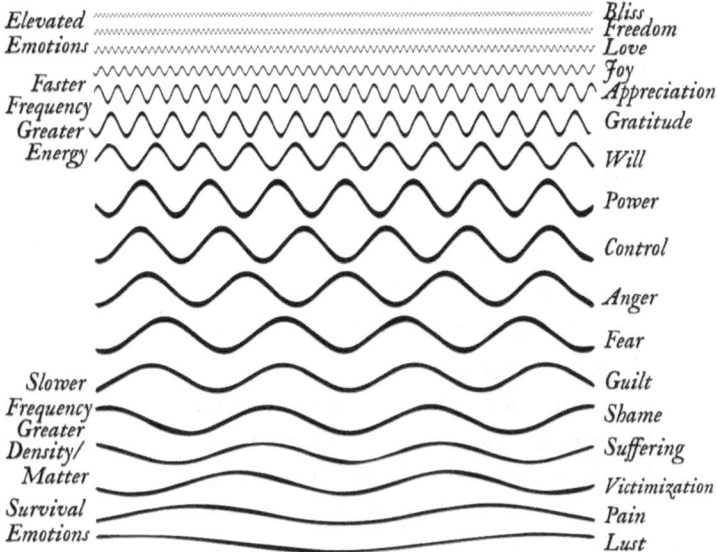

Our thoughts and emotions determine our vibrational energy. That energy can be felt by others, but more importantly, that energy is mirrored back to us through the universal law of cause and effect. You'll learn more about the universal laws in the next chapter.

How do we strengthen our brain-heart coherence?

There are many ways that you can strengthen your brain-heart coherence. The most powerful tool is meditation. But many people don't have a clear idea of what meditation really is. So let me make it nice and simple! For the purposes of this book, meditation is simply a way to disconnect from the mind (as when we practise Stone Heart) and to instead connect to the consciousness that sits behind the mind (as when we practise Light Heart).

There are a number of tools that you can access to help you meditate. For example, you can listen to meditation music on YouTube or various meditation apps. I use one called Brain.fm. Brain.fm uses audible beats to tune your brain frequency to different activities, such as focus, relaxation, sleep, or meditation. Listening to audible beats to retune your mind's frequency can snap you out of stress or ego, and help you solve whatever problems you may be facing.

When I meditate, I stick my headphones in and use Brain.fm to listen to a gamma pattern of beats. This tunes my brain to release gamma waves, which are the energy frequency associated with meditation.

Once your brain waves are in sync and you achieve clarity of thought, the next step is to tune in your heart's energy. By adding in a powerful visualisation of a new present moment that you desire along with intense positive emotions, you tune your heart into the same vibrational energy as your brain, creating alignment to self.

For example, imagine you desire love in your life with a significant other. You can clarify your intention through meditation, then start visualising and experiencing those intense feelings of loving and being loved. Hold that visualisation for 30–60 minutes. When you wake up from that meditation, your whole body will be in alignment with love. Your body, your thoughts, your feelings, everything. This alignment is the step needed to manifest a new reality instead of littering your future with patterns of the past.

Strengthening Light Heart is all about practising brain-heart coherence so that you can live from a place of alignment with self.

EMBRACE LIFE AND FIND JOY

When you start to live by the principles of Light Heart, you open yourself up to a rewarding positive feedback loop. Through acceptance of the present moment and brain-heart coherence comes inner peace, and through peaceful acceptance comes yet greater oneness with the present moment as you disconnect from your thoughts and appreciate all that is. Only by surrendering to life can we fully embrace it.

Truly being alive is more than just living. To be alive is to be awake and aware of your every moment. As Eckhart Tolle says, "Joy is the dynamic aspect of being". When you are in beingness, you will have joy. To enjoy life is to be present; in the present moment you have joy. Enjoyment will satisfy your hunger for happiness. That's not to say you shouldn't strive to learn and grow and achieve great things. It only means that you are not linking all that growth, achievement and success to your joy. You can have joy separate from your trophy collection (or lack thereof). It's the journey that matters, not the destination.

While it is possible through presence and acceptance to find some joy in every moment, of course there are some activities that bring more joy than others. To expand your joy, recognise what these activities are. Maybe it's exercise, reading, or playing with the kids. Whatever it is, do more of it!

On the other hand, mundane tasks like taking out the rubbish or cleaning the toilet may strip you of joy. When you feel this way, bring your awareness into the moment and be alive. Your joy will return. It's inherently joyful to remember that you are alive.

My husband and I have spent every waking hour together since the day we started our business. People often question how we are able to be married and also work together. The answer is simple: by being present and having joy. Love can bridge any disconnect and heal any problem – if we let it.

Let us consider how we can bring joy to a vocation or job. When you enjoy an activity you do at work, rather than just doing it as a means to an end, a deep sense of aliveness and joy will flow through you. Again, most of this joy comes from being present with our work. This builds a connection between your inner power and your outer positive action, which will bring powerful results and in turn enable career growth.

A dedicated musician enjoys their present moment so much that their beingness is visible to the viewer. We, the viewers, are often deeply impacted by this; their tangible presence can even move us to tears. The arts have a lovely way of bringing us into the present; we often forget our thoughts for the time that we are appreciating them. We love music because it has the capacity to make us feel pure, unbridled joy.

Having joy means being out of your head and in your heart. It means carrying out even the most mundane tasks in a way that encourages connection with your aliveness. You don't feel alive in your head, you feel it in your heart. Whenever you want to bring yourself back to the present, put your hand on your heart, and repeat this mantra:

I am alive. I am alive. I am alive.
I am well. I am well. I am well.
I am alive. I am alive. I am alive.
I am here. I am here. I am here.
I am. I am. I am.

PASSION AND EMPOWERED ACTION

Passion and ambition are not ego. They are joy and purposeful action on turbo charge. When you find out what your purpose in life is and you couple that with the actions that bring you joy, your energy in those aspects of your life expands into a deeply fuelled passion that drives empowered, thoughtful action. But you must remain focused always on the present moment, and allow your joy to take you naturally towards your goals.

When your final destination takes precedence over your current empowered action, you become stressed. As your focus moves to the potential outcomes rather than the journey itself, the balance between joy and desire falls out of balance. Stress is an indication that you are cutting yourself off from your inner power, diminishing your creativity and ability to manifest.

People who are detached from the destination will remain unperturbed in the face of challenge. They connect with the present moment, are empowered by their passion, and remain detached from challenges along the way. They accept that Rome wasn't built in a day. This is to say, achievement requires empowered action over time. We can't change time, and we can't avoid challenges, but we can choose our empowered actions. This is Stone Heart, Light Heart in action.

STONE HEART, LIGHT HEART

Passion and empowered action bring enormous energy to what you do. You will quickly start to excel as the energy and laws of the universe get behind you. Onlookers will be in awe of your achievements. But don't let that go to your head, or you will lose your power base. You can only truly enjoy your achievements if you do not completely identify with them. The minute you become attached to something, your ego starts to take back over.

Stone Heart, Light Heart in Action

Go back through this chapter and rewrite the parts that resonated with you or underline key 'Aha!' moments.

. . . .

. . . .

. . . .

Reflect on what you have written down and digest your learnings.

Now write down three new behaviours you can implement to develop a stronger Light Heart.

. . . .

. . . .

. . . .

Reality is created in the mind of the viewer. There is no one reality. There are multiple realities all happening at once.

CHAPTER 8

ACCELERATING LIGHT HEART

"...and when you want something, ALL the universe conspires in helping you to achieve it."

Paulo Coelho

What Is Accelerating Light Heart?

Have you ever met someone and thought, "Wow, they had a big energy"? As we have just learned, around every human exists an energy field. The more joy, peace and love you feel, the higher your energy. The more anger, sadness, guilt, or shame you feel, the lower your energy.

Accelerating Light Heart is about understanding that you have that energy, and making it bigger. The only way to do that is to be in states of peace, joy, and love more deeply and frequently. And that in turn means you need complete detachment from your ego – also known as Stone Heart! So now we begin to see how Stone Heart and Light Heart fit together and complement each other.

Once we've understood Light Heart and started to practise coming back to the present, we can accelerate. This is about expanding our energy in a whole range of directions. There are countless ways in which we, as humans, do not currently reach our full potential. Accelerating Light Heart enables access to these new reaches.

Why is accelerating light heart so important?

Every human has a creative centre. You, like everyone else, are a creative being. The world has evolved because human creation has evolved in it.

Expanding your heart energy will give you access to the creative force that resides within you. When you are present and disconnected from ego, the energy that is born from the heart acts as a powerful engine that accelerates your vibrational energy, empowering you to manifest and create your life at a faster rate.

The mind may be vast, but its strength is limited. The heart's energy is subtle and soft, but infinitely stronger. It is only when we bring them both into alignment, however, that we create true power. With heart and mind in alignment, you can say what you mean and think without attachment or judgment. When you feel your mind trying to take over, you can move into a state of detached awareness.

Just as the heart influences the mind, our thoughts and words have an impact on our heart energy. Our own ideas can easily lead us astray from the truth of who we are, so we must be mindful of them at all times. The more you can curb those stray thoughts, the quicker your Light Heart energy will accelerate, and the easier it will become to manifest your desires. It's all about building power from the source energy that sits within your heart.

ACCELERATE LIGHT HEART BY EXPANDING YOUR INFLUENCE

To accelerate Light Heart, we need to work within the laws of the universe. The great scholars, inventors, athletes, and leaders of our time have all mastered the so-called mysteries of life by truly understanding and respecting these laws. In so doing, they have expanded their conscious awareness and in turn increased the energy flowing into their lives. Energy comes in many forms – love, money, health, etc. – and is directly linked to one's consciousness.

LIVING BY THE LAWS OF THE UNIVERSE

Everything has order.

There are twelve constant, immutable laws that govern this universe. These are Mother Nature's rules, and they have been understood and observed by cultures across the world for thousands of years. By understanding how our universe cycles, you can be more purposeful in how you live and more effective in manifesting your desired future.

You'll recognise many of the principles of Stone Heart, Light Heart in the universal laws. As you move towards self-mastery, you may find it useful to return to these laws from time to time as a helpful reminder of how Stone Heart, Light Heart works in practice.

Together with the guides around me, I have worked for many years to achieve a deep understanding of the twelve laws of the universe. Let me explain them to you now.

The law of divine oneness

Everything in this universe is connected to everything else. Every atom is connected to every other atom. I am connected to you. Everything we think, say, do and believe has an effect on others and the universe around us. Even your most private thoughts can be felt on some level by those around you. Manifestation works through the law of oneness. Our great healers also work with the law of oneness. They can channel their energetic healing through thought because they understand that everything is connected.

The law of vibration

Everything in the universe vibrates. Every single atom is moving. Even at a subatomic level, there is movement. At a macro level, every planet and star system is moving. The law of vibration applies not just to our physical world but also to our inner world of thoughts, emotions, and ideas. They are all constantly moving. It is the *quality* of the movement that dictates the vibrational energy. Limiting thoughts and emotions produce sporadic movement and low vibration; higher-quality thoughts and emotions produce consistent movement and high vibration.

The law of rhythm

Everything vibrates and moves to certain rhythms: seasons, cycles, stages of development. These rhythms reflect the regularity of the universe. Masters can rise above drama, surf the waves of challenge, and detach from their emotions because they understand that each is just a cycle. They never get excited or depressed by external cycles, because they know that to do so is to allow the ego to penetrate their consciousness.

The law of gender

The law of gender recognises that all things have both a masculine and a feminine energy. Everything in nature is both male and female, as both are required for life to exist. This law is the foundation of your creative energy, because not only are both masculine and feminine required externally for procreation, they are also required internally for self-creation. You have both masculine and feminine aspects to who you are, regardless of your sex. We get so hung up on gender in our society; I'll talk about it more later in the chapter.

The law of perpetual transmutation of energy

This is a personal favourite. This law talks to the power of high vibrational energy to make positive change to our environments. Higher vibrations consume and transform lower ones; thus, each of us has the power to change the energies in our lives simply by transforming our own energy. This is the core reason why I've written *Stone Heart, Light Heart*. Applying high vibrational thoughts can transform your inner world and then your outer world through these powerful laws.

The law of action
This law is about the correlation between action and manifestation. It states that action must be employed in order for one to manifest their desired reality. You can't just visualise what you want to happen, you need to take relevant actions towards that reality. Visualising your dreams is like pouring fuel into a car – it's a great start, but you still need to drive to your destination!

The law of cause and effect
This law essentially states that nothing happens by chance. Every action has a reaction or consequence. Some people understand this as karma, others say, "You reap what you sow" or "What goes around comes around". This law becomes particularly powerful when you consider that even your thoughts have a vibrational energy. This is why affirmations can be so powerful. Affirmations gradually become unconscious thoughts, and those thoughts drive your actions.

The law of correspondence
The law of correspondence is similar to that of cause and effect, though it is more specific to the relationship between the outer, physical world and the inner, ethereal world. The law of correspondence essentially dictates what we already know to be true: your inner world dictates your outer world. What you think or imagine corresponds to a real and genuine change in your external environment.

The law of compensation
The law of compensation states that when you give to others, you give to yourself. The universe compensates you for the energy, thoughts, love, kindness, money, and time that you give to others with something of equal value, potentially

in a different form. The inverse is also true: when you take, steal, or hurt, you can expect to be hurt in some way in return.

The law of attraction
The law of attraction explains how we create the things, events, and people in our lives. It states that our thoughts, feelings, words, and actions produce energies that attract kindred energies. Negative energies attract negative energies and positive energies attract positive energies. Again, this plays into the idea that your inner world becomes your outer world. It's all connected.

The law of relativity
In the spiritual world, the law of relativity asks you to assess yourself independent of others, in your own reality. Rich, poor, good, bad, beautiful, and ugly are all relative concepts, dependent on comparison. The law of relativity states that no human circumstance is inherently good or bad except insofar as it can be compared to something else. Everything is neutral when viewed in isolation.

The law of polarity
The law of polarity states that everything has an exact opposite: good and evil, happiness and sadness, right and wrong. There is a yin and a yang to all things. This law relates deeply to the human condition and ties in with the law of relativity. For example, we can only experience the depths of sadness when we understand what happiness feels like. Success tastes that much sweeter when you've experienced failure.

These laws exist at the intersection of science and consciousness. Those who truly understand how these laws work and utilise them in their everyday lives are ultimately able to master their consciousness, which in turn provides them with energy, love, hope, and acceptance.

If you were sitting up on a cloud looking at the world below, you would marvel at its magnificence and the oneness of its myriad kingdoms and systems. You would see humans supporting their neighbours and helping humanity push forward with intelligence and love. You would see the drama and harm, the love and fun, and remember that all cycles of life come and go like waves in the sea. You wouldn't judge; you would simply pay reverence to all that is. Accepting and living by the laws of the universe is about taking this view of every moment.

Embracing the feminine and masculine polarities

Gender is a story. It's the story you tell yourself because of your genitals, or more to the point, because of what your society tells you about your genitals. The story may be pushed on you from the moment you are born, when the hospital sticks a little card on your crib with your details. Yes, your conditioning might have begun with the simple assignment of a coloured card – blue or pink. This is not necessarily a bad thing, nor a good one. But it's important to be cognisant that your conditioning started pretty early.

There is a subset of people who don't connect with the story given to them. They may have male genitals but connect with a female story, or vice versa. They may feel somewhat more in the middle, or that their gender is fluid.

This section is not about LGBTIQ. It's about how you can work with your consciousness spirit to drive your decisions so they sit *above* your gender.

On International Women's Day, I coined the phrase "My genitals do not define me." And they don't. On a physical level I guess they do, and perhaps on an emotional level to some degree, but on a spiritual level, not at all. When the point of death comes and we reflect on our lives, we do so spiritually, not physically. We ask ourselves, "Did I love enough?" and "Did I live my truth?" not "Was I the best woman I could be?".

Some time ago, a friend of mine came over for lunch. He is a seasoned CEO who now resides in the Middle East, where he runs a huge conglomerate. He is the same age as me and has two small kids. We were talking about men and women in the workplace. He repeatedly stated that he thought men made much better CFOs than women and that he had never met a good female CFO. This amused me to no end. He was definitely telling the wrong person if he wanted agreement with his sexist comments! He went on to say, "Do you seriously think women have the same opportunities as men?".

He was of the opinion that your genitals define you, and that's it. His comments were not grounded in consciousness. They were grounded in anatomy, nothing more. The penis versus the vagina. It's zoo thinking at its most basic – limbic and animalistic. There is no neocortex thinking here. At an animalistic level, women and men are different. At a conscious level, we are not. We can all choose where we want to play and how we want to live out – or not – the story of gender.

The masculine and feminine polarities exist in all of us. The balance of masculine and feminine energy varies from person to person, and the balance is not always reflective of the gender a person identifies with. There is a continuum of masculinity and femininity in every human. For example, in Western society we call males at the masculine end of the continuum "alpha males" and those at the feminine end "SNAGs" (sensitive new-age guys). They're all males physically, but energetically it is clear that they are on opposite ends of the continuum.

As you awaken to your power, it's important that you awaken all aspects of your power, both feminine and masculine. It's your birthright to expand consciousness in both. When I work with people, I help them see how their polarity could be out of balance and I help them become more whole in both their masculine and feminine energies. True femininity is not a rejection of all things masculine, just as true masculinity is not a rejection of all things feminine. Our role is to embrace both masculinity and femininity in ourselves, to master both so we can live a well-balanced life.

Effortless flow

Effortless flow is a state of being where things in your life happen more easily, where being in the present moment is maintained without conscious effort. Ultimately, this happens as a feature of being detached from your ego, and connected instead to the moment itself. Your work towards detachment allows for the expansion of your consciousness.

The effortless flow experience is powerful enough to change your universe. When you're in perfect alignment with your vision, and you trust that things will come together for you through the laws of the universe, huge things will happen. When you live with Light Heart, that energy creates and manifests into actual meaningful change.

I experienced this personally as I went through our recent business merger. Like many industries, recruitment was hit hard by COVID19. Initially, we had to cut the size of the business in half. Yet throughout that time, I focused on envisioning the new business. It was a process of saying to myself, "Reo will rise out of the ashes into something completely new". Instead of just accounting and finance, we've now built a business with a plethora of divisions.

Even in the realm of sports, which is probably the domain where we recognise "flow" most easily, we can go much further. Flow as we commonly think of it is no more than a moment, a brief period of the game where our body does what it needs to without us having to even think about it. But imagine if it wasn't just a moment. Imagine if you could spend the entire game in effortless flow.

Here's the thing: you can. When you master Stone Heart and are living out of Light Heart, there's an expansion of energy in your life that sustains long periods of flow state.

True effortless flow is not just a moment in time. It's a series of moments, an opening up to something bigger.

Manifesting Your Own Future

Did you know you are capable of psychic intuition?

There's no such thing as predicting the future, so don't get hung up on that! The future is not written. You may argue that the sun will always rise, and I am not contesting the patterns of the universe! I am simply saying that there is no way to predict the future because, like the past, it doesn't exist. There is only the present moment. The past exists only in our memories and the future exists only in our fantasies – which is to say, each exists only in our present. And we each write our present moments from one to the next.

By sharpening your methods of perception – your five senses – you can increase the accuracy with which you read your energetic field in your present moment, and this means you can essentially create the next moment. Your energetic field is a personal data set so rich in information about the present moment that by mining that information you can become "psychic". You can know what the immediate future holds, because you are the one making it happen. Call it your sixth sense.

So how do you tune into your energetic field? By meditating and going beyond the mind to embody your true self. Know thyself. This is really step one to self-mastery.

Know thyself, to thyself be true.

Enter the cockpit of your life, where you are the sole pilot. In the cockpit, your energies, your thought patterns, and your life purpose are all right there in front of you. Your cockpit has all the controls, communications, and location equipment… but it doesn't have a predetermined flight path to follow. So what direction do you want to go in? What do you need to do to point yourself in that direction?

The path to the future is paved in the present. We cannot know for certain the next step we will take in the future, but we can choose the direction we are facing in the present. This is a key area where people give away control. Next time you find yourself worrying, don't think, "This person's going to be angry at me" or "This terrible thing is going to happen". Instead, choose to pave a path in a direction that favours the solving or removal of the issue at hand. Often you will find that the issue can be entirely resolved in the present, preventing its continuation into the future.

Change your future by changing your present. Accept responsibility, detach from your ego, and live your life in control.

There is no such thing as a psychic ability to read the future. However, there is a such thing as mastery of your own energy, and when you can create your energy field, you can create and manifest your next moment. That renewed next moment is, in essence, your future. Manifestation of the future happens when you set your own flight path.

Don't ask yourself what your future holds (the answer is obvious: whatever's in your energetic field). Ask yourself whom you need to be and what you want to manifest.

Manifestation is about connecting to your energy source and utilising its power. The less connected you are to thought, the more connected you are to heart, and the higher your vibrational energy. Your energetic frequency will therefore increase steadily as you practise Stone Heart, Light Heart. And as your frequency gets higher, so will the speed with which you can manifest.

The effects of energy are visible everywhere in nature: in the waves of the sea, the movement of leaves in the wind, the destruction of a forest by heat, the shattering of glass by sound.

And they're visible in the workplace, too: when a colleague greets you in the corridor, you can immediately sense whether or not they are present by their tone and demeanour. A person who is present relays an energetic power that radiates positivity. A person who is not present could give you a sense of stress or even disdain. In every moment, you can choose whether or not to bring your presence forward.

Consider your energy and the impact that it is having on the forms around you. Are you in manifestation mode or are you in destruction mode?

Above all else, manifestation calls upon a supportive state of consciousness. It doesn't matter what you do, if your state of consciousness doesn't support your goals you will not manifest. Your state of consciousness directly correlates with your energetic vibration. What you do is always secondary; who you truly are is primary.

Stone Heart, Light Heart in Action

Go back through this chapter and note the parts that resonated with you or underline key 'Aha!' moments.

. . . .
. . . .
. . . .
. . . .
. . . .

Reflect on what you have written down and integrate those the learnings.

Now write down three new behaviours that you can implement to have an accelerated sense of Light Heart.

. . . .
. . . .
. . . .
. . . .
. . . .

I master my inner world so I can master my outer world.

Chapter 9

Leading with Light Heart

"CEOs are hired for their intellect and business expertise – and fired for their lack of emotional intelligence."

Daniel Goleman

What Is Leading with Light Heart?

Leading with Light Heart means understanding that energy is contagious and your energy in any given moment will set the tone for your team.

Mastering Light Heart is not just about the personal benefits, it's also about the advantages you can bring to your team if you practise and share Light Heart with them.

As a leader, having time and space for connection is imperative to your wellbeing but also to your energetic leadership practice. You are your team's energy source, too. Great leadership extends past frameworks and giving people clarity. As useful as these can be, they are only useful if you also have high vibrational energy as a leader. Great leadership from a resonant energetic being is infectious and supports people to step up into positive energy. To have positive energy, one must detach from thought and simply observe the present moment.

The responsibility is all yours. That's why leadership is so hard. Leadership is about looking in the mirror and going deep into yourself to ensure that you are mastering the *I* within. How can you coach others to master themselves if you can't master yourself? Mastering the *I* within puts you in a strong position to lead others because when you understand how to master yourself, you can support others to do the same.

Why is leading with light heart so important?

It doesn't surprise me at all that a poor relationship with the manager is one of the most commonly cited reason for leaving a job.[14] A poor employee-manager relationship can lead to a raft of issues including lack of motivation, gossip, and underperformance.[15] If we're seeing a trend towards technology usurping actual people in businesses it's not because "the robots are taking over", it's because humans haven't mastered their own senses of self. At least with robots you know what you are getting! With humans, it's a game of chance.

Good leaders have such a strong inner vibrational energy that their team members will mirror it regardless of how they felt when they first stepped into the office. If you are a leader with strong vibrational energy, you'll pull others up into the same vibrational plane. This is why even a quick 15-minute chat with a great boss can completely change your mindset for the day. It's not just about clarity and solving problems. It's about energy.

Smart, sharp executives don't seek coaching in how to run a business. They seek coaching in how to be a good leader. Good leaders are worth their weight in gold.

If you awaken your Stone Heart, Light Heart, you will be a powerful leader, as your vibrational energy will shine like a light, attracting people to you and brightening their reality.

My team will mirror my vibrational energy.

LEAD WITH LIGHT HEART BY FOCUSING ON YOURSELF

Sounds counterintuitive, right? But when you think about it, of course good leadership starts with you. Leading with Light Heart means that you strongly value your leadership capacity and understand that it will improve as your energy and self-knowing grows. We must allocate regular time in our schedules for habits that encourage this growth.

To lead with Light Heart, you must develop the habit of coming back home to yourself. You can do this through meditation, exercise, gardening, or any activity where you can naturally be fully present.

As a leader, my Stone Heart, Light Heart practice is my number-one priority every day because I know that this is how I will become a better individual. And I know that this will come more naturally and consistently if I turn it into a habit. Each day, I approach my work with the same attitude: I will be detached. I will have high vibrational energy. My team will mirror that energy and grow in their understanding of how their own energy impacts others around them in both good and bad ways.

Find the Inner Space

Underlying our personality is an aliveness, a presence, a consciousness. This is the life behind the ego. This is Light Heart.

Busyness is a place of obligatory one-thing-after-another-ness. Every day, we have many new ideas, which our egos attach to and depend on for our sense of identity. But these ideas are not who we are. This busy place is not one of consciousness and awareness, it is merely a paradigm.

Space or inner stillness is often relegated to a place of secondary importance in our day-to-day lives. But if there is no space between your thoughts, then you are not connected to the present or the spiritual dimension. Constantly listening to your thoughts, one after another, is a new-world definition of insanity.

You must build your awareness of being conscious by bringing your attention to the space between your thoughts. By expanding the space between your thoughts, you'll find a deep sense of peace. If you don't learn to pay attention to this space, you will be constantly at risk of losing yourself to external situations or even to your own mind.

Next time you feel angry or scared, stand back and observe your emotions. This simple act of observation is synonymous with presence. As long as you are observing your ego's reactions, you can be detached from them, which allows you to regain control. Even the observation that you are out of control paradoxically demonstrates some degree of control; you are deliberately exercising your presence and awareness. This is powerful. As you sit in your awareness, you must maintain objectivity in your observations. The moment you move from objective observation to subjective judgment, you drop back into your ego. Observation is the opposite of judgment.

THE FREQUENCY OF LEADERSHIP

As a leader, your inner state of consciousness determines your vibrational frequency, which in turn sets the energy of your team. You've heard it a thousand times, but I'll say it again: Leadership comes from within.

It wasn't until my mid-thirties that I truly started to embrace my leadership responsibility. It took me until then to thoroughly understand and accept that what's happening in my outer world – the behaviours and energy of my team – is a direct reflection of what's happening in my inner world. When you lead, you set your team's vibe, velocity, and intention for the day, week, month, and year. This in turn determines the direction your business takes – your strategy, your game plan, your vision. It all starts with you.

The best book I have read on leadership is Daniel Goleman's *Primal Leadership*, in which he shares the science of what happens to the minds and bodies of people who are in harmony.[16]

He references studies that show when an individual is in hospital, their vital signs including blood pressure, heart rate and metabolic rate all improve when a loved one is present in the room with the patient. What does this mean? Love, energy, confidence, connectedness all have a physical impact on the human body. We impact each other at a cellular level every day. Secondly, it showed that when two people are in rapport, the human body responds by de-stressing.

The opposite is also true.

If you do not have a good rapport with someone, your body will release stress hormones. Your heart rate will increase, you'll feel tense, and you might even need to rush to the toilet as the adrenaline sends your body into a fight/flight/freeze frenzy.

How does your team respond physically to you as their leader? Do you send them into limbic states of stress, or do you support them to be their best, calmest selves?

Your frequency is your leadership.

There was a time when my leadership wasn't consistent and my energy would wax and wane. Working with my spiritual coach has helped me to build my leadership. With her coaching I have awakened my Stone Heart, Light Heart. I have overcome stories, judgments, fears, and the pain I used to associate with failure. I have more joy and I am cognisant that my number one job as a leader is to set a strong vibrational tone. When you ascend into a higher consciousness (spirit, mind, and emotions), so does your team. Leadership is a spiritual game. This book can't teach you the outcome, it can only show you an entry point to the experiences and the choices that will create that outcome. It is up to you to turn inward and take control of your leadership with Light Heart.

When I began leading my business, some people thought energy and spiritual reflection was woo-woo or voodoo. I was the subject of much judgment and mockery. Those people left the organisation, as they didn't align. Now, when a team member achieves a goal, they attribute it to their vibrational energy. After a failure, they heal the disconnection and disappointment with Stone Heart. When something magical happens on the floor, it's not uncommon to hear, "The universe delivered today!". This is a reflection of my personal leadership style. You will also have your personal style. Build your style by turning in and growing the consciousness within.

Detach from your mind's stories

If leadership is about your frequency and how you hold your energy and thoughts together, it's also about how you manage the stories in your mind.

Say there is a small altercation in your team. Two team members are upset and come to you, each complaining about the other. Most people would judge each side of the story, take a side, and choose a winner. But you are not most people! By picking a winner, you challenge the loser's ego. So how else can you approach the problem?

Leading with Light Heart means becoming aware of your mind's stories in these moments and noticing your emotions. This is the first step to successfully resolving conflict: finding a place of objective awareness. If you can disconnect from any egoic stories and instead search for the facts, you're in with a much better chance of solving the problem. Once you have understood the facts of the situation, you can use these facts to illuminate the best solution and move on. This way, you are all winners. The only thing that's been lost is the problem.

So long as your energy remains consistently calm and free of judgment, your team will naturally reflect that energy and connect back to performance. This is Light Heart leadership in action.

BE THE CHOSEN CHIEF

In tribes and indigenous communities across the globe, people are often led by chiefs. The chief is not only the person who heads up the tribe, they also run the community, guiding it to work as a team. Members of the community live together but also work together to care for children, harvest food, and build better communal facilities. These communities run in a similar way to corporations in that every person is designated a job. For the chief, that job is to lead.

Usually, the chief is an elder and is often democratically chosen by the community. Chiefs are calm and wise, and they are practising students of their wisdom. They can be relied upon to interpret the needs of the people and make decisions that will keep them safe and happy. They've been around the block enough times to make the right decisions to solve the community's problems. The chief is the prime minister, the police constable, the priest, and much more all in one.

The chief of a tribe has a beautiful energy. They are tough, fearless, hopeful, and confident. They practise the wisdom of the laws of the universe and make centred decisions in the face of challenge because they are calm and at peace. They have Stone Heart.

The role of the chief is of utmost importance to the survival of a tribe. And this is just as true in a corporate "tribe".

In a corporate setting, a chief is a team leader, manager, group manager, or chief executive. The ultimate chief in an organisation is the CEO, but there are chiefs at every tier of the hierarchy. Each chief sets the energy and therefore the performance of their team. When the chief is a strong leader and understands the universal laws, the team is resonant and performs well. When the wrong chief is chosen, the team loses connection and impact. Motivation plummets, performance drops, and people start to resign.

Ultimately, the effective chief will be the one up for promotion, because they have proven that they can lead well and maintain high vibrational energy in themselves and in their team. When they achieve that promotion, they will be granted more people to lead (and more money!), thus advancing business performance even further.

I have been in recruitment since 2007 and have seen this process happen many times. People choose jobs according to the chiefs, and people leave jobs according to the chiefs. We are familiar with the idea that the chief is chosen, but we are less inclined to consider that chiefs are also *un*chosen. Often, when a CEO of a company moves on, a number of top executives resign shortly afterwards. It's not explicitly stated, of course, but they are in effect unchoosing their new CEO.

As a leader, your people will choose you. If you lose people from your team, investigate their choice – was it related to you, their chief? Sometimes it won't be, but often it will.

As the chief of your team, ask yourself:

- ❖ Am I the leader I wish I could have?
- ❖ Have I won the hearts of my team?
- ❖ Are we in harmony?

The chief knows who they are. They don't play games of double-meaning, of playing both sides, of hedging their bets. They give direction and provide wisdom to those seeking answers. Leading with Light Heart means putting your wisdom into action. It starts with you walking the walk, setting the example. When you implement high vibrational energy in your own life, your team (whether it's your family, your staff, or your squad) will follow.

Be the chief people choose.

Stone Heart, Light Heart in Action

Awaken your Stone Heart, Light Heart now. Look around you. Observe your team members' behaviours and states of consciousness. What are they reflecting back to you? Are they resonant beings?

Write what you perceive. Which of these perceptions are reflections of you?

. . . .
. . . .
. . . .
. . . .
. . . .
. . . .
. . . .
. . . .
. . . .
. . . .
. . . .
. . . .
. . . .
. . . .
. . . .
. . . .

Are you the leader you wish you could have? What do you want in a leader? Reflect on what you have written and notice any gaps you can work on.

. . . .
. . . .
. . . .
. . . .
. . . .
. . . .
. . . .
. . . .
. . . .
. . . .
. . . .
. . . .
. . . .
. . . .
. . . .

SECTION THREE:
POWER

I am, that I am.

Chapter 10

Power

"Whatever the mind can conceive and believe, the mind can achieve."

Napoleon

STONE HEART, LIGHT HEART

Mastery of Stone Heart and Light Heart is your power. Combining detachment and infinite love with courage and energetic propulsion is the foundation of your great inner power. Power begins with mastering the inner world. If you can take back control over your thoughts and your body through the techniques of meditation, you will slowly start to master your external world.

In the beginning, all your attention should be directed towards mastering Stone Heart. As you master Stone Heart and claim the canvas of your mind, a freedom will come over you. You will come to realise that you really can control your destiny using your mind. As you build awareness of the old habits and limiting beliefs that have been bringing you down, they will begin to drop away. The simple act of bringing awareness to your old habits or beliefs will be enough to stop the brain from firing in that old pattern. You will cut the old circuitry and rewire your brain for good!

Light Heart will then help you lay new foundations based on the vibrational energy of joy, love, and acceptance – the highest and most powerful vibrational energy in creation. For the first time, you will be in control. You will silence the voices in your head and write your own flight path. From this place, you will connect directly with your source energy. Instead of hoping to achieve something, you will apply your wisdom to manifest it. You will moderate your electromagnetic waves and own your electromagnetic field, and in this way, you will choose the way your future plays out. With absolute control over your own vortex of energy, you will consciously create a high vibrational energy that resonates with those around you to bring their energy up to the same level. You will tune into the reciprocal energy of the universe and accept the positive energy flowing into your life. Like attracts like. You get this now.

Life will start to feel light, more in flow, more enjoyable. Your health will be better, you will rarely get sick, and your immunity will be strong. You'll start to notice little synchronicities in life, like people calling you when you think of them, or bumping into someone that you really needed to see. Life will begin to move in mystical ways that seem like coincidences – but in truth they are not. They are manifestations in your field.

The inner work that you do on yourself will become the most important part of your day. You will prioritise it because you know that this is what sets you up for mastery. You will use it to create your destiny through conscious thought and choice.

You are a powerful being. To realise that power is your birthright. Own it by becoming a master and a practitioner of connecting mind and body through resonant energy.

Finding Power Through Purpose

When I notice a fly in my backyard, it's invariably an annoyance. It buzzes around aimlessly, sitting on my food, flying in my face, bothering me and generally making a nuisance of itself. When I notice a bee, on the other hand, I feel differently. It's essentially doing the same thing – buzzing around my backyard – but it's doing it for a reason. The bee is looking for flowers to pollinate so that it can take that pollen back to the hive and turn it into finger-licking good honey. The bee has a purpose in life. It is a key part of the flowering cycle and it also is part of the alchemy of turning pollen into honey. The bee is a magnificent and purposeful creature. And it will sting you if you're not careful. It has boundaries, and there are consequences if you cross those boundaries. You know where you stand with a bee. The bee is consistent and purposeful.

Are you a bee or a fly?

Are you driven by a reason for being?

We all have a purpose – a unique code and script that defines where we find meaning, fun, and happiness. It's just a question of whether you have discovered what that purpose is.

Often, your purpose is found in the things that give you the most joy, which can only be experienced through presence and awakened consciousness. When we experience joy through awakened consciousness, we are driven to do that same thing over and over, which ultimately leads to mastery. This is how people find hobbies and passions. It's where they find the energetic propulsion to do something magnificent. Purpose is linked to your present moment.

How to find your purpose

Your purpose is essentially your life's vision. How you get there is your mission.

Your vision might be to reduce national poverty. Your mission will be *how* you intend to make that impact – for example, by rising up the political ranks in order to put forward proposals for better public housing or higher welfare payments. This is what will get you out of bed every day. It's the doing rather than the being.

To define your purpose, you need to do the work. I did a great exercise (below) with a thought leader called Glen Campbell who runs a program called Brandheart that helps executives define their personal brand[17]. Defining your life's vision, mission, values, key personality traits, and key signature behaviours helps you define the framework by which your best self can be born.

For me, defining my purpose started with reflecting on the following questions:

- ❖ What do I like about myself?

- ❖ What don't I like about myself?

- ❖ If I knew I was going to die in six months, how would I live my life (assuming I still had to work and my environment wouldn't change)?

- ❖ How will I live my life as it stands?

- ❖ Do I have a hero – dead or alive, real or fictitious? What character traits do I love in them? What is it about them that I wish I could have?

- ❖ Write your eulogy as if you had led your fullest life and lived out your deepest desires.

Often the best way to find these answers is through facilitation, but you can definitely start to unravel them yourself. All these questions, and therefore your answers, are interconnected. After you have completed this exercise, you will begin to see a few themes around your vision and mission. These themes lead you to your purpose. It's that thing that you are here to do, contribute, experience. What is your vision for your life here on Earth?

A purpose isn't a strategy for you to become rich. No matter where you are in life, you could be living out your purpose. Your purpose shouldn't change even if your life circumstances change. It's an ethos of who you are and how you want to live out your life. This also can't be a goal that requires time to achieve, as you need to be able to live your vision irrespective of money or environment. This is not to say that you can't have a vision around reducing poverty. It means, however, that your vision is not focused on the completion of this ideal, but on the action of that ideal.

Let's look a little deeper at question three, so as to gain greater understanding of how to work through these questions. Asking yourself how you'd live your life if you only had six months left is a way of coming closer to the things that are a priority for you. Likely, in answering this question, you'll prioritise the things that bring you joy, and the things that bring you meaning. It may be spending time with family. It may be writing a book. Often the answer to this question fuels the continuation questions: why wouldn't you do these things? Why wouldn't these things be your focus still, if you had longer to live?

These questions, when they're done properly, are a full-day exercise. What this activity is showing you is that you're going to have a gap. When you compare what you'd do with six months left, versus how you live life now, you'll find gaps. These are the differences between what you want and what you're currently doing. What is in those gaps is important, and should be part of your forever. Often the things you find are the very things that bring enjoyment. They may be little things, but they are integral parts of your purpose.

For me, it was the answer to question five that really got to the heart of my purpose. The hero question asks you to identify who is a superhero in your life. When I stopped to think about that, no one came to mind, because I'm not one who idolises superheroes. Yet I heard a whisper in my mind that said, "Oprah, Oprah, she's your hero." I thought, how ridiculous. But I went with the thought. If it was Oprah, what was it about her life that was important to me? What I identified in Oprah is that she was always seeking wisdom. She was always chasing knowledge from people around her, around self-mastery and around living a more wholesome life. What got me thinking even further about her was that she made it her personal purpose to share that with the world. Her interviews were mainly geared to sharing the learnings, the wisdom and the opportunities that people faced, so that we all could learn and grow as a human race.

Oprah goes out and gets the wisdom, and she applies what she learns. As a result, she's become someone who is having a huge impact on our global intelligence. That's my interpretation of what she does, anyway. Does that mean she actually does that? Maybe, maybe not. It doesn't even matter. The point here is that there is something in what she does that resonates with me, something I want to emulate. I want to practice what I learn, I want to practice what I preach. There are some activities that she has done in her life that I want to do in my life. It's not about Oprah herself, it's about what *I* see in Oprah. That's what the activity does for people. It's an articulation activity. It's about identifying the behaviours and traits you desire so you can see what your purpose is.

My purpose is to practise wisdom to shed light in the world. This has always been my purpose, even if I didn't always realise it. This purpose has taken me into medicine, NLP, and recruitment, and has led me to become a practitioner of spirit. This book is itself a physical manifestation of my purpose: practising wisdom to shed light in the world.

No matter what moment I am in – home life, mum life, work life – I am able to draw on my vision and know that I am on purpose. I hold space for my vision in my present moment at all times so that I can live my vision in everything I do. Even if I am in a crappy place, I always come back to my vision. So long as I am living life as an extension of that vision, I am on track. The key thing is remembering that living your purpose is not necessarily about how you earn – or spend – an income. It's where you spend your time, where your joy comes from. For example, if your purpose has something to do with one of the global sustainability goals, you'll likely align yourself to an organisation that is dedicating itself to that cause. You might donate anything from your time, your thinking, your reading, or your energy.

My mission is to awaken people to the infinite possibilities around them. This is how I will live out my vision: by awakening others to the infinite, by sharing teachings in the areas of consciousness and the practice of personal and spiritual awakening. This book is a piece of learning material that I will use as a teaching aid to fulfil my vision.

The exercise above is repeated at the end of the chapter for you to complete in order to define your purpose. Create an open working document that you can refer back to and refine over time. As you go through the motions of life, the happiness and sadness, the success and failure, the excitement and fear, you will know that, no matter what, you are clear on your vision and your mission. The rest you can detach from and let be.

WHAT IF YOU COULD?

With every human being born, our collective consciousness moves a step forward. As time passes, we are becoming more intelligent and less violent. More empathetic and less animalistic. We are in a time now where people are more aware than ever of their own consciousness, and we are increasingly realising that our collective mission is to increase the resonance of our collective consciousness. We *can* live in harmony with one another.

B1G1 is a philanthropic organisation that helps not-for-profit organisations across the globe connect with givers that want to make a difference. Aligned to the UN Global Goals, B1G1 has helped thousands of people make micro donations to projects in communities they otherwise wouldn't have known existed. Though each donation may be small, together the impact they can have is huge.

I have spent some time with the chairman of B1G1, Paul Dunn, and I know that a hallmark of his conferences is that he always poses the same famous question:

What if?

What if we could eliminate poverty across the globe?

What if every child could have an education?

What if every human had access to clean drinking water?

What if?

What if you could master your life by mastering your mind and thoughts? What if you learned the craft of think and create? What if your word was your wand? What if you could heal the wounds of your past and rewire your brain with new, more constructive pathways? What if you could heal your body?

What if?

Self-mastery takes persistence and dedication. It's a choice you need to make based on your personal values in life. Self-mastery is a way of life. A way that will set you free from control and bring you true freedom.

This journey is not an easy one. It will require focus and attention. The way will unfold for you step by step. Be patient and kind to yourself. Every awakening you have will layer upon the last. As you grow in your awareness of yourself, your power will also grow.

Be courageous. Let your failures make way for new learnings. Be open to the knowledge and wisdom that come with those learnings.

With wisdom comes freedom. All will be yours when you are wise to all that is. With wisdom comes love. Love for self, love for humanity, love for all that is. Love is an all-conquering force that heals and takes us forward through life.

My wish for all humanity is that every person is able to embrace the power of the human spirit by mastering their inner world.

Live a bigger life. Open your mind to the infinite possibilities that surround you. The infinite is waiting for you to tune in and bring it towards you. Keep it simple. Don't overcomplicate this. Just get in and get the work done. Your heart's intelligence will show you just how powerful you are and how worthwhile it can be to master your mind, your body, your life, and your spirit.

Namaste.

Stone Heart, Light Heart in Action

Find your purpose. Ask yourself:

What do I like about myself?

. . . .
. . . .
. . . .
. . . .
. . . .

What don't I like about myself?

. . . .
. . . .
. . . .
. . . .
. . . .

If I knew I was going to die in six months, how would I live my life (assuming I still had to work and my environment wouldn't change)?

. . . .
. . . .
. . . .
. . . .
. . . .

How will I live my life as it stands?

. . . .
. . . .
. . . .
. . . .
. . . .

Do I have a hero – dead or alive, real or fictitious? What character traits do I love in them? What is it about them that I wish I could have?

. . . .
. . . .
. . . .
. . . .
. . . .

POWER

Write your eulogy as if you had led your fullest life and lived out your deepest desires.

. . . .
. . . .
. . . .
. . . .
. . . .

Reviewing all the information above answer the following questions:

What is my vision for my life here on Earth?

. . . .
. . . .
. . . .
. . . .
. . . .

What is my mission? How will I achieve my vision?

. . . .
. . . .
. . . .
. . . .
. . . .

STONE HEART, LIGHT HEART

What will the outcome of your vision and mission be?

. . . .

. . . .

. . . .

. . . .

. . . .

REFERENCES

[1] Massey, M. E. (1979). people puzzle, understanding yourself and others. Reston Pub. Co.

[2] Dilts, R. B., Grinder, J., Bandler, R., DeLozier, J., & Cameron-Bandler, L. (1980). Neuro-linguistic programming (Vol. 1). Meta.

[3] Patterson, K., Grenny, J., McMillan, R., & Switzler, A. (2012). Crucial conversations tools for talking when stakes are high. McGraw-Hill Education.

[4] Hewitt-Gleeson, M. (2000). The X10 Memeplex: Multiply Your Business by 10!. Pearson Education.

[5] Cardone, G. (2011). The 10X Rule: The only difference between success and failure. John Wiley & Sons.

[6] Duckworth, A., & Duckworth, A. (2016). Grit: The power of passion and perseverance (Vol. 234). New York, NY: Scribner.

[7] Baer, D. (2014, May 1), 'This is the personality trait that most often predicts success', Business Insider, https://www.businessinsider.com.au/conscientiousness-predictssuccess-2014-4, accessed March 5, 2021.

[8] Goleman, D., Boyatzis, R. E., & McKee, A. (2013). Primal leadership: Unleashing the power of emotional intelligence. Harvard Business Press.

[9] Frankl, V. E. (1985). Man's search for meaning. Simon and Schuster.

10. Dispenza, J. (2017) 'The Generous Present Moment: A Guided Meditation', Meditation download https://drjoedispenza.com/products/the-generous-presentmoment-by-dr-joe-dispenza-meditation-download
11. Koran, A. (1964). Bring out the magic in your mind. Embassy Books.
12. McCraty, R., Atkinson, M., Tomasino, D., & Tiller, W. A. Research Library.
13. Dispenza, J. (2019). Becoming supernatural: How common people are doing the uncommon. Hay House.
14. Seek (n.d.) 'The top 5 reasons people leave their jobs', https://www.seek.com.au/career-advice/article/new-research-reveals-the-top-5-reasons-people-leave-their-jobs, accessed March 5, 2021.
15. Teoh, K. R. H., Coyne, I., Devonish, D., Leather, P., & Zarola, A. (2016). The interaction between supportive and unsupportive manager behaviors on employee work attitudes. Personnel Review.
16. Goleman, D., Boyatzis, R. E., & McKee, A. (2013). Primal leadership: Unleashing the power of emotional intelligence. Harvard Business Press.
17. Campbell G, Brandheart, https://brandheartmethod.com/f/bsi/sp-direct/, accessed May 17, 2021.

Acknowledgements

This book has been two years in the making. I want to acknowledge my husband for his unwavering belief in me to pursue my calling. You are the stem that allows this flower to constantly be in bloom. I love you.

To my parents, Harry and Maria; I believe we choose our parents. I chose you, Bubbu, for the spark of wisdom that set my journey on course. I chose you, Mum, for your love and nurture.

To my sister and brother for being in the grandstands always cheering. You are my biggest fans.

I'd like to acknowledge Marcela; my multidimensional teacher, sister and dear friend. You have been my greatest teacher on this journey of self-mastery. You are one of my favourite gifts from the universe. Namaste and thank you.

I'd like to acknowledge Alena Bennett, Leadership coach and advisor, for helping me breathe life into this book and for being a strong influencer in my life as a CEO.

To my group of chiefs in my CFO and CEO consortiums, you have been my board and helped me materialise the concepts of Stone Heart, Light Heart in the business world. Thank you.

To my team at Reo Group, you reflect back to me the aspects of myself that I need to master. You are the best mirror for self-development and self-mastery. I am forever grateful to those who have come and gone, and those who have stayed. Namaste.

To my business partners at Reo Group. I stand on your shoulders. You lift me high above the clouds. I see a great vision and a wonderful story to be told in a future book. I love doing business and sharing this journey with you.

ABOUT THE AUTHOR

Stella Petrou Concha is the inspiring co-founder, CEO, and driving force behind fast-growing brand Reo Group. Her mission is to elevate human potential by working with executives to deliver value for their organisations through talent selection, leadership, strategy and vision.

After commencing a career in medicine, she quickly realised the medico-patient care dynamic was never going to meet her need and lifelong goal to help people on a deeply personal level. Instead, she discovered a powerful alignment with the recruitment and management consulting sector.

Stella founded Reo Group in 2009, and the business has won many industry awards since. She was named one of Australia's Top 10 Female Entrepreneurs in 2018. She currently chairs for CEO consortium '2020 Exchange' and is an advisor to many C-suite professionals, boards and executives in the Australian Business Community.

Through her energy, intuition, and vision, Stella brings a unique and powerfully human perspective to the Australian talent sector.

Stella is the co-author of *Legacy – The Sustainable Development Goals in Action* and *Stone Heart, Light Heart – The Intelligence of Self Mastery.*

Stella's mantra is, "When you succeed, I succeed".

stellapetrouconcha.com.au

Putting Stone Heart Light Heart Wisdom Into Practice

Ready to master yourself and bring forth your inner power?

To complement this book I have created a Stone Heart Light Heart Digital Workbook, exclusive to my book readers, to help you record your progress as you work through some of the lessons I have created.

Scan the QR code below to download the workbook and start your journey of self mastery!

www.ingramcontent.com/pod-product-compliance
Lightning Source LLC
Chambersburg PA
CBHW021434080526
44588CB00009B/525